Date Due

DEC 15 1994		
JAN 2 3 1996		
---DEC 1 8 997		
NOV 2 3 1999		
FEB 2 4 2011		
SE 0 9 15		

CANCER:
CAN IT BE STOPPED?

Dr. Alvin and Virginia B. Silverstein

New Revised Edition

J. B. Lippincott   New York

Illustrations on pages 18, 22, 32, 81, 88, and 103 by Patricia Tobin.
Photo credits: Photomicrographs by Dr. Gilla Kaplan, Department of Cellular
Physiology and Immunology, The Rockefeller University, New York, New York
10021, 5, 71, 83, and 99; National Cancer Institute, 20, 24, and 35; National
Institutes of Health, 61; Centers for Disease Control, 75; Genentech, Inc., 85;
courtesy of authors, 104.

Cancer

Designed by Bettina Rossner
10 9 8 7 6 5 4 3 2
Second Revised Edition

Library of Congress Cataloging-in-Publication Data
Silverstein, Alvin.
    Cancer: can it be stopped?

    Summary: Explains the various forms of cancer, their
symptoms, possible causes, and treatment; and discusses
research being conducted to find better means of pre-
venting, detecting, treating, and curing this disease.
    1. Cancer—Juvenile literature. [1. Cancer]
I. Silverstein, Virginia B. II. Title. [DNLM: 1. Medical
Oncology—popular works. QZ 201 S587c]
RC263.S49 1987   616.99′4   86-45500
ISBN 0-397-32202-X
ISBN 0-397-32203-8 (lib. bdg.)

*To the memory of Representative John Fogarty,
who did much to foster medical research.*

Acknowledgments

The authors would like to thank Dr. Sumi L. Koide of Rockefeller University for her careful reading of the manuscript and her many helpful suggestions. Grateful acknowledgments are also due to all those who so generously supplied information and photographs, especially Adele Paroni of the American Cancer Society, Dr. Gilla Kaplan of Rockefeller University, and Maggie Bartlett of the National Cancer Institute. Thanks, too, to our editor, Christiane Deschamps, for her capable assistance, support, and patience.

Contents

CANCER:
CAN IT BE STOPPED?

1. Cancer: The Most Feared Killer

Cancer is one of the most dreaded of all diseases. It can strike young or old, rich or poor. No country in the world is spared from its terrors. In the United States, cancer is the number-two killer, second only to heart disease.

The name of the disease *cancer*, like the sign of the Zodiac with the same name, comes from a Latin word meaning "crab." If you picture a crab, its legs and claws seem to spread out from its body. Cancer, too, can spread out, invading the normal tissues and organs of the body, choking them off and destroying them. Cancer may bring with it terrible pain, far worse than the most agonizing pinch of a crab's claws.

One of the most frightening things about cancer is that it is a disease in which the body's own cells seem to turn traitor. Somehow the cells forget the jobs they are supposed to do and instead begin to multiply wildly.

This year, more than 450,000 Americans will die of cancer. And each year, the number of cancer deaths increases. Although cancer is mainly a disease of older people, it strikes many young people too. In fact, cancer is the second most common cause of death among children, after accidents. Twenty-eight out of every one hundred Americans can expect to come down with cancer at some time in their lives, and about eighteen of them will die of it. This is a disease that involves almost every American family.

Researchers are fighting back against cancer, and much progress has been made. Of the one million people who will be diagnosed as having cancer this year, nearly half will still be alive five years from now. According to estimates by the American Cancer Society, hundreds of thousands more could be saved, even with the treatments now being used, if they were diagnosed early enough and treated promptly. New studies, still at the laboratory stage, could save even more lives. The National Cancer Institute has recently proposed a goal of cutting the cancer death rate by 50 percent by the year 2000.

Calls for a national goal of stamping out cancer may sound

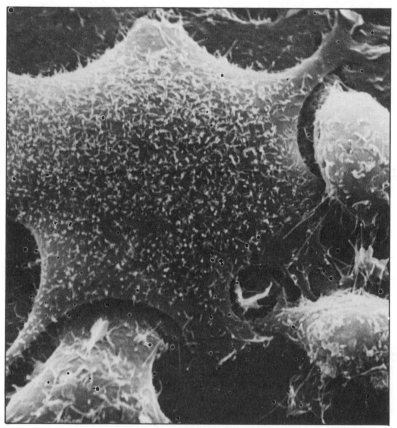

L929 mouse tumor cells invading a culture of mouse macrophages. (The cells on the left and top, under the tumor cells, are macrophages.) This photo, magnified 3,300 times, is a scanning electron micrograph (SEM). It is built up in much the same way as a television picture, by a finely focused beam of electrons moving across the surface of the specimen. SEMs provide a dramatic three-dimensional picture of surface details and are useful in studying a cell's interactions with its environment.

familiar. Back in 1970, the U.S. Congress unanimously re-
solved that the disease should be eliminated "by 1976, as an
appropriate commemoration of the two-hundredth anniver-
sary of the independence of our country." In December
1971, President Nixon signed the National Cancer Act, which
declared war on cancer. Over the years that followed, billions
of dollars were poured into cancer research. Some of the
money was used to improve the treatment and care of cancer
patients. Much of it supported studies of the causes of cancer
and new ways to treat it. Discouragingly, the numbers of
cancer deaths continued to rise with each year. Yet there
were also reports that the new treatments were helping cancer patients to live longer, and giving them better chances
to survive.

A debate has been raging recently over what the cancer
statistics mean. "Cancer: No Longer a Death Sentence"
headlined the views of many specialists. Yet other experts
have made headlines of their own, claiming that "We Are
Losing the War Against Cancer." How can the same numbers be interpreted so differently?

It is true that the numbers of new cancer cases and cancer
deaths have continued to increase steadily in spite of our
"war on cancer." But there are some explanations. First of
all, the average age of the population has been increasing
steadily. Medical advances have brought new treatments and
cures for other diseases. Consequently, people who might
have died of pneumonia or heart disease or kidney failure

are now living on to the ages when they are more likely to come down with cancer. Smoking is another important factor: Medical experts point out that without the deaths from lung cancer, due mainly to smoking, the cancer death toll would actually be going down.

What about the fact that cancer patients are living longer after diagnosis? Certainly that is encouraging. Well, some critics point out, we may be fooling ourselves with that sort of statistic. New tests and techniques are permitting doctors to diagnose cancer at an earlier stage. Are today's treatments more effective, or are patients surviving the same amount of time but just knowing about it longer? The optimists on the cancer scene say that the latter may be true about certain types of cancer, such as lung cancer, but that we have made real progress in treating some other types, such as breast cancer and leukemia. In addition, they argue, numbers don't tell the whole story. Today's cancer treatments are better, even if they don't keep patients alive much longer, because they give patients a much better quality of life—without the disfiguring and disabling major surgery that used to be the only treatment available.

There is another important factor that today's cancer statistics do not take into account. We are just at the beginning of a revolution in medical research. Sophisticated new techniques are permitting scientists to copy nature's chemicals and to tailor-make new chemicals that never existed before. Scientists have new means of introducing drugs and biological agents into the body and are on the verge of learning to change hereditary instructions to correct nature's mistakes. In addition to these new biomedical tools, there has been a revolution in cancer research itself. For the first time, scientists have a theory that explains many puzzles of what causes cancer and suggests new approaches to treating and curing it. According to this *oncogene* theory, normal cells that make up our bodies contain within them some *genes*— bits of hereditary information—that have the potential to turn into cancer genes.

Cancer research is a long and often discouraging process. Often you will see reports in the newspapers of an amazing new cancer cure, and then you may never hear of the new wonder drug or technique again. Some of the new "cures" turn out to be good only in the test tube or culture dish; others work on animals but not on humans. Some of the new approaches do turn out to be valuable additions to the cancer doctors' arsenal. But their development takes many years. Researchers have to be very cautious: New treatments are tried first on animals, then on a small number of people under carefully controlled conditions. It must be established that they are both effective and safe. Often new or controversial cancer treatments are tried out on people who are in the late stages of the disease, with the rationale that they are doomed to die anyway and have little to lose, even if the treatment should turn out to have harmful side effects.

But such studies can be misleading: The body may be so weakened by the disease that nothing could save it. The development of some promising treatments has been delayed because of disappointing results of early tests on terminal cancer patients.

When a treatment seems to be effective, researchers must be equally cautious about their conclusions. It is difficult to keep from getting excited when a cancerous tumor shrivels up and disappears as though by magic, and a patient who seemed to be dying is restored to vigorous health. Yet experienced doctors know that sometimes that sort of "miracle cure" can happen spontaneously with or without any treatment. In addition, cancer is an insidious disease. It can flare up, then seemingly disappear, going into *remission*. The patient seems to be cured, but the disease is still lurking and may appear again, perhaps in a different part of the body, weeks or months or years later. In evaluating new treatments, cancer researchers may be encouraged by immediate effects, but they are not confident they really have something valuable until they find out whether their patients are still alive and healthy two or three or five years later. Only then can the new treatments be used widely.

Cancer specialists have found that once a cancer patient has been cancer free for five years, there is an excellent chance that the cancer will not recur; therefore many cancer statistics include five-year follow-ups. Thus, today's cancer statistics are not an accurate reflection of what is currently going on in front-line cancer research. They are the results of treatments being used five years ago or more.

Treatment is only one part of the war against cancer. Another important feature is prevention. Medical experts are growing more and more aware that environmental factors and aspects of our life-style can help to cause cancer. Cigarette smoke and air pollution, certain chemicals produced in factories, certain foods we eat and drugs we take, radiations such as X rays or even too much sunlight—all may work to change normal cells into cancer cells. By changing various aspects of our life-style, we can play a big part in the 50-percent reduction in cancer deaths by the year 2000 projected by the National Cancer Institute.

Before exploring the current theories on what cancer is and how it develops, as well as the ways it can be treated or prevented, we must first find out more about how the normal body works.

2. The Human Body

A human being is a most wondrous thing, able to dream and plan, smile and laugh, walk and run. The human body is a smoothly running "machine," far more complicated than any machines people have made.

The parts of the body work in a beautiful harmony. Each depends upon the others. The heart pumps the blood that feeds the lungs and the kidneys, the hands and the feet. The lungs, in turn, bring in fresh oxygen that helps to burn the fuel that the stomach and intestines have digested. The kidneys and liver remove the poisons that are formed from the various chemical reactions in the body.

The heart, the lungs, the kidneys—indeed, the whole body—are made up of tiny, living building blocks, the *cells*. Trillions of cells work together in a single human body. They come in a variety of sizes and shapes: Those in the lining of the cheeks look like miniature paving stones. The nerve cells that link the various parts of the body in a communications network look like long threads. The red blood cells that float through the bloodstream look like tiny doughnuts without the hole in the middle.

Each cell is like a busy factory. Thousands of different chemicals react with one another to form new substances that help the cells to live and do their own special jobs. Nerve cells carry messages that permit us to see and hear and think. Muscle cells work with nerve cells to help us move. Red blood cells carry oxygen to all the other cells of the body. White blood cells help to fight infections.

Each cell is surrounded by a very thin covering that is like a plastic bag. This is the *cell membrane*. It is a rather unusual covering that lets only certain chemicals through and keeps out others. Some scientists think the cell membrane plays a very important role in cancer.

The inside of the cell is divided into many compartments by a network of membranes that branch off from the cell membrane. Within these compartments is a fluid called the *cytoplasm*, which contains chemicals and various tiny structures.

The *nucleus* is a structure inside the cell that controls many of the cell's activities. Inside the nucleus is a substance called *DNA*, which contains genetic information for the body, organized in units called genes. These genes contain the complete plans for the body. Genes determine whether you will have blue eyes or brown, whether you will have two legs or four, hair or feathers or scales. Genes send out information that tells the cell what chemicals to make, as well as how much and when to make them.

In the nucleus, the genes are joined together, like beads on a chain, into structures called *chromosomes*. A normal human body cell has forty-six chromosomes, which contain an average of several thousand genes each. During certain phases of the cell's life cycle, the chromosomes are stretched out into long, thin strands, and they are tangled together into a network called *chromatin*. At other times each individual chromosome is condensed into a separate, rodlike structure, which can be seen clearly under a microscope. In addition to DNA, the chromosomes contain proteins, some of which cover the genes that are not "turned on" at that particular time.

Information is carried out into the cytoplasm by partial copies of the genes' DNA, constructed from a related chemical called *RNA*. The form of RNA that carries the DNA message is called *messenger RNA*. It interacts with two other forms of RNA, found in the cytoplasm: Various forms of *transfer RNA* pick up amino acids, the building blocks of proteins, and carry them to structures called *ribosomes*, which have their own *ribosomal RNA*. The ribosomes are the cell's protein factories. Their RNA acts as a platform on which amino acids, brought by transfer RNA, are assembled into proteins according to the blueprints provided by messenger RNA. Thus the original genetic information, stored in a coded form DNA, is carried out of the nucleus by RNA and then translated into proteins. Some of these proteins form body structures; others are *hormones*, chemical messengers that help to coordinate body activities; still others are *enzymes*, chemicals that help to control and direct the body's chemical reactions.

Even when the growth of the body as a whole has ended, many of the body cells continue to grow and multiply. Skin cells on the surface of the body, for example, are continually being worn away and replaced. If part of your liver were damaged by disease, the remaining liver cells could grow and multiply to replace the damaged part. When a body cell reaches a certain size, it divides to form two perfect, smaller copies of itself. Each of the new *daughter cells* receives a complete set of genes, carrying all the hereditary instructions. The growth and development of the cells follow very strict rules. A skin cell, for example, will produce new skin cells, not eye cells or heart-muscle cells.

According to current theories, cancer occurs when something changes the DNA in a cell to activate the oncogenes. Instead of sending out the signals for normal growth and development, oncogenes carry instructions that cause cells to grow and divide more rapidly than normal cells. Dozens of oncogenes have already been isolated, and their protein products have been determined. Some of these are enzymes, which cause biochemical changes in other protein molecules that change their activities and the cell's behavior. Others are DNA-binding proteins that may act directly on particular genes and turn them off. Still others have structures and activities very similar to growth hormones or the structures on the cell surface (*receptors*) that interact with them and give chemical instructions that tell the cells to grow. Researchers are still working out the details of how these effects of oncogenes make cells cancerous. Some give cells the ability to go on growing indefinitely; others affect the way cells interact with their neighbors. Typically, each oncogene causes many changes in a cell's structure and behavior.

When a cancer cell divides, each of its daughter cells receives a complete set of genes—including the activated oncogenes that prompt them to grow furiously, too. Soon a growing mass of cells forms, crowding out the normal body cells. This is cancer.

3. What Is Cancer?

Cancer is growth run wild. This growth is similar in some ways to normal growth in the healthy body. The cells get larger and, when they reach a certain size, divide in two.

Normal cells stop growing after a while or grow only at a rather slow pace. Cancer cells do not necessarily grow faster than normal cells, but they continue to grow under conditions when normal cells would stop. Researchers have observed in laboratory experiments that when the cell membranes of two normal cells touch each other, both cells stop growing. Somehow each gives the other a signal that turns off the DNA that controls cell growth and division. Scientists call this exchange of signals *contact inhibition*. But when two cancer cells touch, somehow the stop signal is not given or is not received properly. The DNA is not turned off, and the cancer cells continue to grow and divide. They pile up in an untidy heap, one on top of the other. They can even invade nearby normal tissues. Normal cells are held together by a sort of glue. But cancer cells give off, or secrete, a certain chemical that seems to dissolve the glue. Then the cancer cells can squeeze in among the normal cells and spread through them. They form a growing lump of cancerous tissue called a *tumor*.

Actually, "tumor" is a general term for a swelling in the body. Some tumors are not cancerous. For some reason, cells multiply for a while, but then the tumor stops growing when it reaches a certain size. The cells begin to obey the normal contact signals again. A tumor that stops growing in this way is called a *benign* tumor.

But some tumors continue to grow and spread. These cancerous growths are called *malignant* tumors. They may grow to the size of a grapefruit or larger. The original microscopic cancer cell must grow and divide, doubling many times to form such a large tumor. It takes about thirty doublings to produce a mass about one centimeter in diameter. Usually tumors that form deep inside organs cannot be detected until they reach about a one-centimeter size. If the tumor is a slow-growing one, it may have taken several years to reach that size.

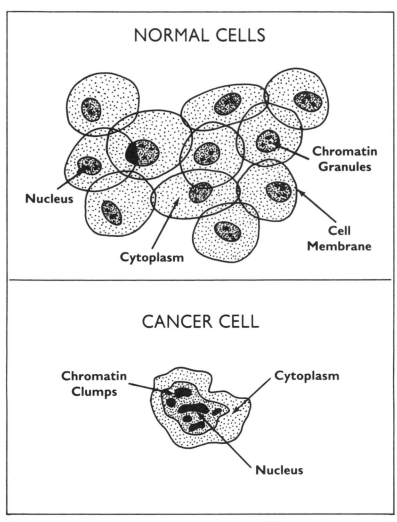

Under a microscope, a cancer cell reveals many differences from normal cells, including an enlarged nucleus and an irregular shape.

As a cancerous tumor grows, its cells become wilder and more disorganized. They may lose their normal distinguishing characteristics and become *dedifferentiated*. Whether they originally started off as skin cells or brain cells or liver cells, eventually they just look like very abnormal, cancerous cells.

Another important difference between cancer cells and normal cells is that cancer cells don't seem to stick together as well as normal cells do. Often single cancer cells or clumps of them will break away and be carried along in the bloodstream or lymph channels. These cancer cells may settle in other parts of the body and begin to grow there, too. This migration of cancer cells through the body by way of the blood and lymph circulation is called *metastasis*.

Cancer kills by invading and destroying normal tissues. Key organs of the body, such as the lungs or intestines or liver, may be blocked or damaged so badly that they can no longer do their work. Cancers that have metastasized—spread through the body—are the deadliest. Surgeons may be able to remove the main tumor completely, or various other treatments may be used to destroy it; but the small secondary tumors are still lurking in other parts of the body, and the treatments may not reach them.

How does cancer get started in the first place? What changes a well-behaved normal cell into a wild, uncontrollable, destructive rebel? We don't have all the pieces of the puzzle yet, but scientists now believe that they will eventually all fit into the oncogene theory.

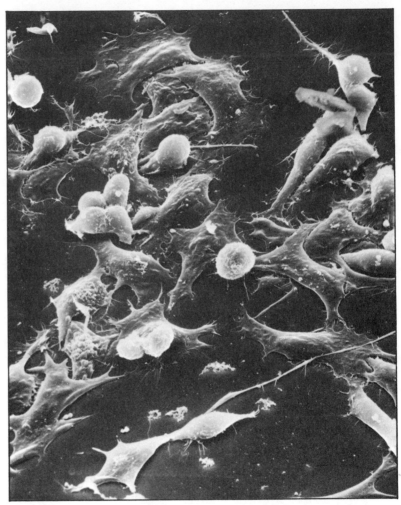

Scanning electron micrograph of a Wilm's tumor (a human carcino-sarcoma). Typically the cells are round, but when they attach to a sur-face they spread out.

According to this theory, humans and other living creatures carry within their cells a number of genes potentially capable of causing cancer. These oncogenes normally exist in a harmless, turned-off form. Perhaps at some stage of life they play a key role in the cell's chemical reactions, probably concerned with growth and development. But once their job is done, they are switched off again and remain quiet—unless something happens to activate them.

Oncogenes can be activated in various ways. Recent studies have found that 70 percent of oncogenes are located near weak points on chromosomes—hereditary regions where the DNA molecule may break, or portions of it may be rearranged into new combinations. Such damage to the chromosome might remove the oncogene from the influence of the genetic control mechanisms that normally govern its action. Or an inactive oncogene might be moved next to another gene that has an activating effect. Indeed, many researchers believe that the formation of a cancer cell is a complicated process requiring at least two oncogenes, which must cooperate, each playing a different role.

A number of chemical substances can produce breakage, rearrangement, and various other changes in DNA that might activate an oncogene. (Chemicals that cause cancer are referred to as *carcinogens*.) Radiations can produce similar effects. Viruses may also play an important role in activating and even creating oncogenes.

A *virus* is the simplest kind of living thing, so streamlined

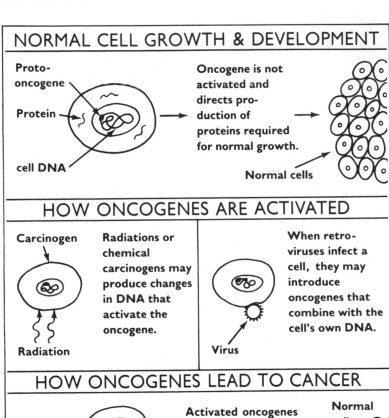

NORMAL CELL GROWTH & DEVELOPMENT

Proto-oncogene

Protein

cell DNA

Oncogene is not activated and directs production of proteins required for normal growth.

Normal cells

HOW ONCOGENES ARE ACTIVATED

Carcinogen

Radiations or chemical carcinogens may produce changes in DNA that activate the oncogene.

Radiation

When retroviruses infect a cell, they may introduce oncogenes that combine with the cell's own DNA.

Virus

HOW ONCOGENES LEAD TO CANCER

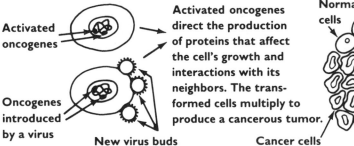

Activated oncogenes

Oncogenes introduced by a virus

Activated oncogenes direct the production of proteins that affect the cell's growth and interactions with its neighbors. The transformed cells multiply to produce a cancerous tumor.

Normal cells

New virus buds

Cancer cells

that it cannot even grow or reproduce on its own. It consists of an inner core of hereditary instructions, spelled out in *nucleic acids* and wrapped in an outer coat of protein. Some viruses contain the nucleic acid DNA, like the DNA in the nucleus of human cells. Other viruses have a different type, called RNA. (In human cells, remember, portions of the DNA in the genes are copied out in the form of RNA and used as patterns to construct proteins, according to a complicated "genetic code.")

Some scientists claim that viruses are not truly alive, since they do not show the normal characteristics of life unless they are inside a living cell of some host, such as an animal or a plant. When a virus invades a cell, it may immediately take charge. It makes the cell its slave, somehow forcing it to stop its own normal chemical activities and instead turn out copies of virus particles. The DNA of a DNA virus acts like a gene, providing the blueprints for the new set of reactions. In some RNA viruses, the RNA provides the blueprints from which the cell produces more virus proteins and copies out more viral RNA. But for RNA viruses of the group called *retroviruses*, the situation is a bit more complicated. *Retro-* means "backward," and retroviruses reverse the usual DNA–RNA sequence. These RNA viruses have a special enzyme called *reverse transcriptase*. With the help of this enzyme, the viral RNA is used as a model for the manufacture of a matching set of DNA, which can then act as a gene.

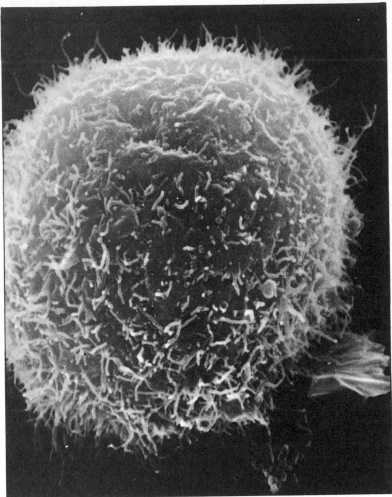

This HeLa cancer cell has been infected with adenovirus. Its rough surface, visible on the scanning electron micrograph, is due to the virus infection.

Sometimes a virus's nucleic acid does not do anything after it enters a cell. It (or a portion of it) may attach itself to the cell's own DNA, or it may remain hidden among the cell's genes—perhaps for years. Using a technique called *molecular hybridization*, researchers have been able to find "virus footprints" in cancer cells. At first they worked with animal cancers that were known to be caused by viruses. Working with a gene called *src*, from a virus that causes a type of cancer called sarcoma in chickens, they found very similar genes in a variety of animals and even in humans. Further experiments revealed that these *src*-like genes are not virus genes but genes of the cells themselves. It is thought that the original cancer-causing *src* gene was a cell gene that an invading virus picked up and carried off when the infected cell produced a crop of new virus particles.

The first human oncogene was isolated in 1981 from a bladder cancer. Since then about thirty more have been found in cancers of the lung, colon, breast, and lymph system, and their positions on the chromosomes have been mapped. In laboratory experiments, these oncogenes have been found to transform normal cells, growing in culture dishes, into cancer cells. Researchers believe that there are probably between thirty and fifty oncogenes in a normal human cell (out of the fifty thousand or so genes that the cell contains).

Meanwhile, other studies have shown that at least four common viruses can cause cancer in humans. Papilloma viruses, which cause warts, can also lead to cancer of the cervix. The hepatitis B virus, which produces a serious liver disease, seems to be the cause of the epidemics of liver cancer that are now raging in many Third World countries. Epstein-Barr virus, a member of the herpesvirus family, causes infectious mononucleosis but has also been linked to several kinds of cancer, including a cancer of the white blood cells called *Burkitt's lymphoma*. Some recently discovered viruses called HTLV viruses cause leukemia. Both Epstein-Barr and HTLV-I viruses have been found to contain oncogenes, which may contribute to the resulting cancers. Researchers think the discovery of virus-caused cancers is especially exciting because *vaccines* against virus infection can be produced. Now that viruses have been linked with cancer, it is hoped that vaccines against such viruses may protect people against at least some forms of cancer as well.

4. Kinds of Cancer

As common as cancer is—striking almost all the animals and plants in the world—it still holds many mysteries.

Cancer takes many forms—more than one hundred in humans alone. Many researchers believe that what we call "cancer" may actually be a number of different diseases, all sharing the characteristic of uncontrolled growth. Others feel that it is a single basic disease, producing a variety of effects depending on what kind of cell it attacks. It can strike almost any part of the body: skin, lungs, intestines, breast, brain, mouth, bones, or blood. Although the same basic mechanism may start off the cancerous transformation of different kinds of cells, the cancers that result behave in practice like many different diseases, with their own characteristic growth rates, patterns of metastasis, and responses to treatment.

In general, cancers fall into three main classes: carcinomas, sarcomas, and leukemias.

A *carcinoma* is a cancer that starts in covering tissues. It occurs in the skin and the inner and outer coverings of the breathing passages, lungs, and the digestive system, from the mouth down through the stomach and intestines. Cancers of the brain, nerves, liver, glands, and some kinds of bone cancers are also carcinomas.

A *sarcoma* is a cancer that begins in connective tissues found beneath the skin or between and within organs and glands of the body. Sarcomas are found in cartilage, a tough gristle that gives shape to your ears and helps to support the bones of your spine. Tumors of muscle and fatty tissue are sarcomas. This type also includes some bone and nerve cancers.

Leukemias are the blood cancers. In these cancers, the body makes too many white blood cells. In the normal body, there is only about one white blood cell for every seven hundred red blood cells. When a person has leukemia, the blood may have as many as ten, twenty, or even one hundred white blood cells for every seven hundred red blood cells.

Both the red and white blood cells are made by red bone marrow cells inside the hollows in some of the bones. In leukemia, some of the bone marrow cells become malignant.

They divide again and again, producing far too many white blood cells. The normal job of the white blood cell is to fight invading microbes. Yet leukemia patients are very susceptible to all kinds of infections. The reason for this is that many of the leukemic cells do not function normally. So although such patients have too many white cells, they do not have enough "working" white cells. Meanwhile, the cancerous bone marrow cells spread and crowd out the normal bone marrow cells, some of which make red blood cells. That is why leukemia patients suffer from *anemia*, a lack of enough red blood cells, which causes weakness and fatigue. The cancerous cells also interfere with the production of blood platelets, tiny structures that function in blood clotting. As a result, the patients bleed easily. For these reasons, they must receive many blood transfusions.

About twenty-five thousand Americans get leukemia each year, and about 10 percent of these are children. A number of drugs and other treatments have been developed for leukemia. Some of the most effective ones cause the leukemic cells to disappear from the blood. This kind of temporary recovery from cancer is called a remission. It may last for months or even years, but often the cancerous bone marrow cells begin to multiply wildly again. Unless the doctors can produce another remission, the patient dies. Progress in the treatment of certain types of leukemia has been dramatic, especially for the forms affecting children. In some medical centers, 75 percent of child leukemia patients are saved. Now there are a number of leukemia patients who have lived for twenty years or longer in a state of remission and seem to be cured.

Most cancers are what are known as *solid tumors*. In other words, the cancer is a solid mass of tissues. When cells become cancerous, they lose many of the normal cell functions and become simpler in some ways—dedifferentiated, as scientists call it. But often they keep a number of characteristics of the original cells from which they developed. A tumor that arose in an endocrine gland, for example, might continue to secrete its typical hormones. If the cancerous tumor metastasizes, the new little tumors that grow in other parts of the body may continue to secrete characteristic hormones or abnormal ones that could serve as the basis for a diagnostic test.

Solid tumors can appear in almost any part of the body. In women, they occur most often as solid lumps in the lungs, in the breasts, in the large intestine (the colon and rectum), and in the uterus, the organ where a baby develops before it is born. Doctors advise women to check their breasts for lumps every month. Techniques such as *mammography* (a form of X-ray testing of the breasts) can be used if cancer is suspected. Yearly mammograms are also recommended for women with a higher than average risk of developing breast cancer: those with a close relative who has had breast cancer. (For others, doctors recommend having a baseline scan by age fifty to establish the normal pattern and then having mammograms every three to five years.) There is a very simple, safe, and effective test for cancers of the uterus. This is called the *Pap smear*, from the name of George Papanicolaou, who developed it. The doctor wipes the cervix (the entrance to the uterus) with a small cotton swab. Thousands of cells that have already broken away from the tissues are picked up on the swab and placed on a microscope slide. A special dye or stain is added so that the doctor can see the cells better under a microscope. If cancer is present, some of these cells will be cancerous, and they will look quite different from the normal cells. In fact, specialists can even detect *precancerous* cells—those that do not look quite normal but do not have all the typical characteristics of cancer cells. With the latest treatments for breast cancer, about three quarters of the patients survive for at least five years. The treatments for uterine cancer are equally effective. In both cases, the earlier the cancer is detected, the better the person's chances of survival. When cervical cancer is detected in the precancerous stage, the survival rate is nearly 100 percent.

In men, cancer occurs most often in the lungs and in the prostate gland, one of the male sex glands, found near the bladder. Cancer of the colon and rectum is also common among men. Sudden changes in bowel habits, abdominal discomfort, and blood in the stools are warning signs of colorectal cancer. These symptoms may be caused by *polyps*, benign growths on the wall of the intestine, or by malignant

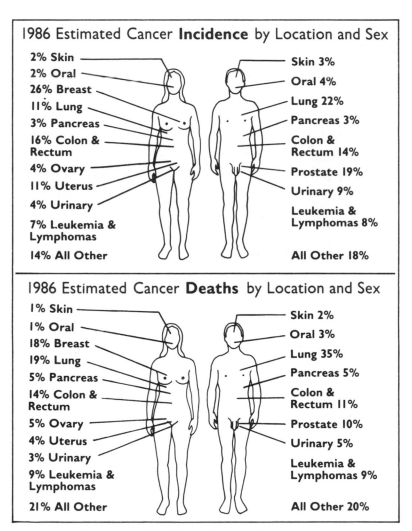

1986 Estimated Cancer **Incidence** by Location and Sex

2% Skin
2% Oral
26% Breast
11% Lung
3% Pancreas
16% Colon & Rectum
4% Ovary
11% Uterus
4% Urinary
7% Leukemia & Lymphomas
14% All Other

Skin 3%
Oral 4%
Lung 22%
Pancreas 3%
Colon & Rectum 14%
Prostate 19%
Urinary 9%
Leukemia & Lymphomas 8%
All Other 18%

1986 Estimated Cancer **Deaths** by Location and Sex

1% Skin
1% Oral
18% Breast
19% Lung
5% Pancreas
14% Colon & Rectum
5% Ovary
4% Uterus
3% Urinary
9% Leukemia & Lymphomas
21% All Other

Skin 2%
Oral 3%
Lung 35%
Pancreas 5%
Colon & Rectum 11%
Prostate 10%
Urinary 5%
Leukemia & Lymphomas 9%
All Other 20%

Cancer statistics, as of 1986. (Nonmelanoma skin cancer is not included.) Adapted by courtesy of the American Cancer Society, Inc.

growths—cancers. They are diagnosed by examining the patient's large intestine with a long, flexible tube called a *colonoscope*, and by a special type of X-ray test called a *barium enema*. (A barium salt is used to coat the wall of the intestine and make it show up better on the X rays.) Survival rates for both colorectal cancer and prostate cancer have been improving steadily over the years, and again, a person's chances are better the earlier the cancer is detected.

Lung cancer kills more men than any other form of cancer—close to one hundred thousand a year. For women, the lung cancer death rate is much lower (about thirty-eight thousand women died of lung cancer in 1985), but it has been climbing rapidly; in fact, lung cancer recently passed breast cancer to become the most common cause of cancer death in women in the United States. Doctors believe that smoking is a major cause of lung cancer, and the smoking patterns among men and women provide a good explanation for the different—and changing—lung cancer death rates. In general, men smoke more than women, but in recent years many men have been giving up smoking while more women are taking it up. There was a much greater difference in smoking habits ten, twenty, or thirty years ago. Since lung cancer develops slowly, often taking decades to appear, the current rates for this cancer still reflect the big differences between men and women smokers in past decades.

Each year, more and more people get lung cancer. In fact, the number of cases of lung cancer is going up much faster than that for any other kind of cancer. Although a cigarette smoker is much more likely to get lung cancer than a non-smoker, some nonsmokers do develop this form of cancer. Part of the explanation is *passive smoking*: A nonsmoker who lives or works with a smoker breathes in some of the exhaled smoke, which contains carcinogens. Air pollution—from automobile exhausts, factory smokestacks, and even natural radioactive gases such as radon—can also contribute to the development of lung cancer.

Doctors used to recommend routine chest X rays for everyone to detect lung diseases such as tuberculosis and lung cancer. Now medical experts advise people to avoid unnecessary X rays; while the tiny amount of radiation in a single chest X ray may not be harmful, many repeated X rays can build up the dose and increase the risk of cancer. So regular chest X rays are advised only for people at special risk, such as heavy smokers.

Some newer tests for lung cancer can detect cancers that might not show up on X ray. Using thin, threadlike *fiberoptic* probes, doctors can actually see down into the lungs. *Sputum cytology* detects cancer cells in samples of sputum coughed up by lung cancer victims and can be used for screening large groups of people. There has been some controversy about how much good it does to diagnose lung cancer early. Lung cancer is one of the most deadly of all cancers, and by the time it is picked up in tests, usually it has spread to other parts of the body too. Studies have shown very little

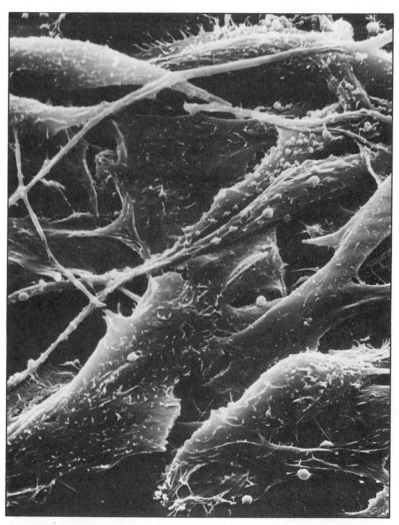

Scanning electron micrograph of a human melanoma, magnified 130 times.

difference in survival rates, regardless of how early the cancer was diagnosed. But some specialists believe that sputum cytology can be used to pick up precancerous cells, identifying the condition at a stage when the victim can still be helped. In fact, it has been found that if a smoker quits smoking, gradually the precancerous cells in his or her lungs turn back into normal cells.

The most common type of cancer in number of new cases is skin cancer, but this is not one of the major killers. About four hundred thousand new cases of skin cancer are diagnosed each year, but only about seventy-four hundred people died of skin cancer in 1985. It is much easier to detect and treat than cancers that occur deep within the body. Many people have warts or moles on their skin. In most cases, these are benign tumors, but they may change into cancerous tumors. Indeed, one of the warning signals of cancer is a sudden change in the size or color of a wart or mole. (Other types of skin cancer may appear as pale, waxy nodules or red, scaly patches.)

The deadliest of all the skin cancers are the *melanomas*. They are cancers of pigment cells, which contain the dark-colored pigment *melanin*. This pigment normally helps to shield the body tissues from the ultraviolet rays of the sun. (When exposed to sunlight, the pigment cells produce more melanin, eventually resulting in a suntan. People with a light complexion do not produce as much melanin as those whose skin is naturally dark.) Melanomas are deadlier than the other skin cancers because they metastasize very quickly to other parts of the body.

People who spend a great deal of time outdoors in the sun have a much higher chance of getting skin cancer. Sailors and farmers are two groups that have higher than average skin cancer rates. The ultraviolet rays of sunlight can produce a suntan or cause a painful sunburn. These rays can also cause *mutations*, or changes, in the DNA inside the cells. Some of these changes can turn a normal skin cell into a cancer cell. But moderate exposure to sunlight—not enough to cause a sunburn—can help to build good health.

Cancer specialists (called *oncologists*) grade cancerous tumors according to how different their cells are from normal cells. (The ones that show the greatest differences and are usually the most aggressive score a Grade IV rating.) They also distinguish cancers according to how much they have spread. A Stage I cancer is just a single tumor at the original site, while in the most serious type, Stage IV, the cancer has metastasized throughout the body. In general, cancers respond best to treatment in the early stages, when their cells have not changed very much from normal cells and before they have spread from their original location. Stage IV cancers are the most likely to be fatal, in spite of all the doctors' efforts.

5. How Cancer Is Treated

During the twentieth century, medical research has led to the conquest of many diseases. The main killers at the turn of the century—pneumonia, tuberculosis, and diarrhea—are no longer feared. Antibiotics and the newer antiviral drugs can bring about dramatic recoveries, and there are vaccines to prevent a number of diseases that used to be widespread. People are living much longer than they used to, and the new major causes of death are diseases mainly of the older years: heart disease, cancer, and diabetes.

Cancer is still a feared killer, but it is no longer an automatic death sentence. We are making steady progress. Back in the 1940's, when penicillin brought the beginning of the revolutionary advances against bacterial diseases, a diagnosis of cancer meant death for three out of four patients. Only one out of four could hope to survive, symptom free, for at least five years after diagnosis, and the main treatment—the only really effective one—was to cut out the cancerous tumor by surgery. Many people feared the pain and disfigurement of the treatment nearly as much as the disease itself. By the 1960's, when penicillin had been joined by a host of new and effective antibiotics, and vaccines were making such diseases as polio, measles, and diphtheria rare, the five-year survival rate for cancer patients had risen to one out of three. Part of the improvement came from the development of better diagnostic tests and procedures, which made it possible to find cancers at an earlier stage. Better treatments were also being developed and tested. The cancer physician could use not only surgery but also radiations and drugs. Now, in the 1980's, the odds for survival have improved still more for cancer patients: Nearly one out of two can expect to survive for five years or more, and can hope for a much healthier and fuller life than cancer survivors of the past. Surgical techniques have been improved, and the combination of surgery with radiation and drug treatments, as well as a variety of immunological approaches that mobilize the body's own defenses against cancer, has made it possible to use much less drastic and damaging forms of surgery. As researchers gain further understanding of the nature and causes of cancer, and new experimental tests and treatments become standard practice, we may at last see a sharp downturn in the cancer death rates.

Surgery is the oldest type of cancer treatment. Ancient records show that Egyptian doctors were using this method to treat cancer about thirty-five hundred years ago. Surgery works best when cancers are discovered early. If a tumor is cut out before it has metastasized, the patient can be completely cured. The reason cancer surgery is often so drastic and disfiguring is that the surgeon tries to get out all the cancer cells, even if this means taking out some of the normal tissues that the cancer *may* have invaded, for if any cancer cells are left they can begin to multiply again after the operation. Consider this: A tumor the size of your thumb contains one *billion* malignant cells. If an operation removed 99.9 percent of the tumor, there would still be one million cancer cells left.

Even if a cancer has spread too far for a cure to be possible, surgery may still help the patient. If a tumor is blocking the intestines or the channels that carry urine, an operation can open the passages, even if not all of the tumor can be removed. Surgery can also help to ease the great pain that cancer can bring.

Cryosurgery—supercold surgery—is a useful technique in the treatment of cancer. Instead of a knife, the surgeon uses a probe with a hollow channel containing liquid nitrogen. Nitrogen, which makes up four fifths of the air we breathe, is a gas. But if it is cooled down to $-320°$ F (about $-196°$ C), the nitrogen turns into a liquid. Liquid nitrogen is so cold that tissues or other substances that come in contact with it freeze rapidly. In cryosurgery, a tumor can be cut out very quickly, with practically no pain or bleeding.

Cryosurgery has some important advantages over ordinary surgery in the treatment of cancer. Less damage is done to the normal tissues, and the wounds heal better. In the ordinary kind of surgery, some cancer cells may break away and travel through the body. They may settle down in other organs throughout the body—the doctor's efforts to help the patient may inadvertently cause metastasis. But in cryosurgery, this usually does not happen. The cancerous tumor is taken out very cleanly and does not get a chance to spread.

Modern surgeons use another weapon against cancer that is almost the opposite of cryosurgery. They can destroy cancer cells with very sharply focused beams of hot light that are made with a device called a *laser*. The colored tumors of melanomas absorb more of the laser light than normal cells do. Thus, the laser beams kill only the colored cancer cells. Dyes that color the cells of other cancerous tumors are being developed so that they, too, can be treated with laser beams. The development of thin fiber-optic probes has made it possible for doctors to literally see into the various tubes and cavities of the body, such as the esophagus, the respiratory passages, and the urinary passages. Probes like these can also be introduced, for example, into the tissues and cavities of the abdomen by way of a very small incision, which will later heal without a large, disfiguring scar. Such fiber-optic probes are not only useful for finding cancers; they can be combined with finely focused laser beams to destroy the cancer cells, vaporizing them right on the spot.

Radiations of various types are very helpful, both in diagnosing cancers and in treating them. You may have had a chest X ray. The X-ray machine was placed against your chest, and invisible radiations called X rays passed through your body. They formed a picture on a photographic plate. By looking at the picture, the doctor can see the lungs and know whether there are any diseased spots or any tumors growing inside them. X rays are also useful for detecting cancer in other parts of the body. Sometimes a chemical that does not let X rays pass is used to outline an organ better in the X-ray picture and thus let the doctor see more clearly whether or not it is completely normal. A person may drink a mixture containing a barium compound for an X-ray examination of the stomach or intestines. The barium compound coats the walls of the digestive organs and makes their details more visible. Or a special dye may be swallowed or injected into the body.

An X-ray diagnostic machine has been revolutionizing medicine. This is the *CAT scanner* (CAT stands for "computerized axial tomography," meaning that computers aid in producing an image as though a cut were made crosswise to the body's long axis). Very narrow beams of X rays are

passed through the patient's body at various angles and recorded with an electronic detector. Gradually a complete
image of a "slice" of the patient is built up, and a computer
uses the information to construct a vivid picture that can
show up tumors, cysts, and other abnormalities. Although
the CAT scan is made from a number of X-ray recordings,
such tiny amounts of radiation are used for each one that
the patient receives no more radiations altogether than would
be used in taking an ordinary X-ray picture. Using the CAT
scanner, doctors can detect cancers deep within the brain or
in organs such as the pancreas, where in the past they were
usually found only by cutting open the patient's body in an
exploratory operation.

The CAT scanner was the first of the powerful new medical
tools provided by modern technology. Now many hospitals
and research centers also have MRI scanners and PET scanners. All these types of scanners are much more expensive
than simple X rays, but they are much more sensitive to
subtle changes in the density and water content of tissues.
Such changes can be used to distinguish between cancerous
and normal tissues.

The *MRI* ("magnetic resonance imaging") *scanners* are
based on the principle of *nuclear magnetic resonance*: In a
field of radio waves, the nuclei of certain atoms act like tiny
magnets and line up all together. If another radio field is
turned on at right angles to the first, the nuclei start to spin
like miniature tops. They wobble as they spin, and after a

while they fall back to their original position. The spinning nuclei send out signals, which a computer can process into a picture.

An MRI scan looks very much like a CAT scan, yielding a picture of a "slice" of the head or body. It is very good for showing up tumors, because the hydrogen nuclei in water molecules send out very strong signals. Since tumor cells do not hold water as tightly as normal cells do, the MRI image shows a distinct contrast between tumors and normal tissues. MRI scans can also pick up some tumors that do not show on CAT scans—for example, those in areas overshadowed by bone, which makes a very sharp image on the CAT scan. But CAT scans are better at showing tumors containing calcium deposits.

A team of researchers from Boston's Beth Israel Hospital and Harvard Medical School has recently reported on a new use of nuclear magnetic resonance (NMR) in diagnosing cancer. They used an NMR spectrometer to test blood samples from 331 people, including some with cancer of the breast, lung, ovary, colon, blood, or other organs; some with benign tumors; some with other diseases; and some healthy volunteers. The NMR measurements detected differences in fat-containing blood substances called *lipoproteins*. Nearly all the patients who actually had cancer showed characteristic changes in the NMR properties of their lipoproteins. (The presence of cancer was determined afterward by *biopsy*, the examination of small samples of suspect tissue under a microscope.) Patients with benign tumors gave a negative NMR test. The only false positives were observed for pregnant women and men with an enlarged prostate. In one patient, the NMR test detected a recurrence of leukemia before any other warning signs were observed. These results are still very preliminary; the researchers do not yet know at what stage the characteristic changes in the lipoproteins show up in the NMR tests. Further studies will be needed to determine whether this new blood test is the reliable early screening test for which cancer specialists have long been waiting.

The *PET* ("positron emission tomography") *scanner*, one of the newest and most expensive of the high-technology tools, gives pictures of the body in action. The positron is a very tiny, unstable particle that is destroyed as soon as it comes in contact with an electron. (Electrons are negatively charged particles found in abundance in all normal matter.) Before a PET scan, the patient is injected with a sugar solution "tagged" with a special radioactive substance that emits positrons. As the radioactive sugar travels through the body, the most active cells take it up. But meanwhile, it continues to emit positrons, which meet electrons and explode, giving off radiations called gamma rays. (The amounts of radiation involved are so tiny that they do not cause any harm to the body.) A gamma-ray detector picks up the radiations, and a computer forms a picture of the scan. Since cancer cells are typically growing very actively, many tumors take up sugar faster than normal cells do. Thus, a PET scan shows tumors in clear contrast to normal tissues.

Radioactive isotopes have been used for cancer detection for many years, long before the PET scanner was invented. Radioisotopes of iodine, for example, are commonly used to diagnose cancer of the thyroid gland, an organ that helps to tell the body how fast to burn its food. This gland contains a great deal of iodine, and when we eat foods containing iodine, this chemical goes mainly to the thyroid. A doctor, suspecting that a patient may have a tumor of the thyroid, can give the patient a mixture containing radioactive iodine to swallow. After the chemical has had time to be absorbed into the bloodstream and distributed through the body, the doctor can move a *Geiger counter*, a device used to detect radiations, over various parts of the body to see just where the radioisotope is. Or the radiations may be recorded on sensitive film, producing a picture called a *scintigram*. The amount of radioactivity in normal thyroid tissue is quite different from that in tumor tissue, and thus the doctor can tell whether there is a tumor in the gland and exactly where and how large it is. Radioisotope scanning can also be useful in detecting metastasis, since secondary tumors in other parts of the body often retain some of the characteristics of the original tumor and may pick up radioisotopes in a similar way. A number of other organs, such as bone, liver, spleen, and lungs, can also be scanned effectively for tumors using radioactive tracers.

The tiny amounts of radiations used in taking an X-ray picture or diagnosing a tumor with radioisotopes are fairly safe (although more and more doctors are tending to feel that even diagnostic X rays should be used only when they are really necessary and not for routine screening). Larger doses of radiations can damage or even kill cells and tissues. They can make changes in the DNA of a cell so that the information it contains is no longer quite right and the cell cannot do its job properly. Radiations can upset the body's ability to make new blood cells and can knock out its disease-fighting cells and organs. They can even cause cancers. But because radiations can kill cells, they provide a powerful weapon against cancer cells. The big problem is to find ways to kill the tumor without killing the patient too.

Cancers of the skin and some other cancers that occur in a small, clearly outlined part of the body can be treated very well with beams of radiations from a machine located outside the body. An X-ray machine may be used, or the doctor may use the radiations from radioactive *cobalt* or some other radioisotope. The beam of radiations can be focused very exactly to hit only the tumor tissue, just as you can focus the spray from a garden hose by turning the nozzle at the end.

A small amount of a radioisotope can also be inserted directly into the tumor. Or the patient may swallow or receive an injection of a radioisotope that will "zero in" on the particular kind of tissue in the tumor. Radioactive iodine, for example, can be used not only to diagnose but also to treat cancer of the thyroid gland, for almost all of it goes to the thyroid gland, and the rest of the body does not receive its radiations. Radioactive *phosphorus* is concentrated in the bone marrow, and is used to treat a rare kind of leukemia called polycythemia vera.

Medical researchers are looking for drugs to use with radiation treatments. They have found some chemicals that cause cells to be more easily damaged by radiations and other chemicals that help to protect cells from radiations. Both types can be useful in helping the radiations to kill off the tumors more effectively and in protecting the rest of the body from damage by radiations while the tumor is being killed. In fact, scientists hope they will be able to find some chemicals that work both ways at the same time, making cancer cells easier to kill and also protecting normal cells.

After surgery and radiation treatments, the next major advance in cancer therapy was the development of *chemotherapy*, or treatment with chemicals or drugs. A number of chemicals have been found to slow cancer growth or to kill the cancer cells, but one problem with most anticancer chemicals is that they are poisonous to the normal cell as well as to the cancer cell. The reason they can be used at all is that many chemical reactions take place at a much faster rate in cancer cells than in normal cells; therefore, the cancer cells take in more of the poisonous chemical than the surrounding normal cells do.

Even with careful adjustment of the dose, all anticancer drugs have side effects that in some cases may be life threatening in themselves. They may damage the bone marrow, resulting in insufficient production of white blood cells and platelets and leaving patients very vulnerable to dangerous infections, even though their cancer may be responding well to the treatment. Other common side effects include damage to the heart and lungs, reproductive disorders, and infections and ulcers in the mouth. Cancer researchers are now searching not only for new anticancer drugs but also for ways of making the existing ones more effective and less toxic.

Modern research in cancer chemotherapy began during World War II. Scientists were experimenting with poison gases. They found that the mustard gas that had been used in World War I could interfere with the growth of cells. A very similar substance, called *nitrogen mustard*, turned out to be an effective drug that is still used to treat certain types of cancer, including some types of leukemia and lung cancer. A newer member of the "mustard" family, *L-PAM* (L-phenylalanine mustard), has been giving good results in the treatment of breast cancer. It is especially useful for women before the age of menopause whose cancer has already spread to the lymph nodes. The mustards, and certain anticancer drugs such as *chlorambucil, cyclophosphamide, nitrosoureas*, and *imidazole carboximides*, belong to a class of chemicals called *alkylating agents*. They all work against cancer cells in the same way: by tying the chains of their DNA molecules together, thus making it difficult for DNA to make the RNA that carries its messages out into the cell. Their action also prevents *DNA replication*, the formation of a copy of the genetic information that is a vital part of cell division.

Another early approach to cancer chemotherapy began in the early 1940's, when Charles B. Huggins of the University of Chicago found that *estrogen*, a female sex hormone, produced remissions of prostate cancer. Hormones are natural body chemicals that act as chemical messengers, traveling in the bloodstream and controlling the activities of cells. Not only estrogen but also other hormones, such as *cortisone*, *prednisone*, *progesterone*, and several *androgens* (male sex hormones), have been found useful in treating some cancers that occur in tissues normally influenced by hormones. In addition, it has been found that in certain cases hormones seem to stimulate the growth of cancers. An excess of female sex hormones, for example, can stimulate the growth of breast and uterine cancers, and injections of the male sex hormone *testosterone* may trigger a long-dormant prostate cancer to suddenly begin growing explosively. Surgical removal of the testes, which produce testosterone, can help stop the growth of prostate cancer and is one of the standard treatments. Drugs that block the action of androgens are also very effective in the treatment of prostate cancer. In 1966, Huggins received a Nobel Prize for his pioneering work on hormones and cancer.

Studies of *antibiotics* have also yielded some drugs that

can be used against cancer. Antibiotics are complicated compounds that are produced by microbes such as molds. Like the first antibiotic, penicillin, most of these drugs are used against bacterial infections; recently, some antibiotics effective against viruses have been discovered. The antibiotics *actinomycin D* and *daunorubicin* are not very effective in treating bacterial infections, for they cause too much damage to human cells while they are killing the bacteria. But they can be used to treat leukemias and some other cancers. *Doxorubicin* (also called *adriamycin*) is an antibiotic that is becoming very widely used against various types of cancers, including leukemia and *osteogenic sarcoma* (a bone cancer that strikes children). Actinomycin D, daunorubicin, and doxorubicin are believed to act by attaching themselves to the cancer cells' DNA, thus interfering with its work.

Alkaloids, produced by plants, are another class of chemicals that is providing valuable anticancer drugs. *Vincristine* and *vinblastine*, products of the periwinkle plant (*Vinca rosea*), work against cancer by acting as *mitotic inhibitors*. The scientific name for cell division is *mitosis*, and these drugs work by stopping cell division.

Another class of drugs that works in a somewhat similar way is a group of compounds containing the precious metal *platinum*. These drugs are picked up by the cancer cells and bind chemically to the cells' DNA, preventing it from replicating (making a copy of itself). The first of these platinum drugs, *cisplatin*, was found to be effective against cancers of the ovaries and testes, certain lung cancers, and a variety of other tumors, but it has serious side effects, especially damage to the kidneys, hearing loss, and severe vomiting. Researchers have been tinkering with the cisplatin molecule, making various changes and testing the effectiveness of new combinations against cancer. They have produced a number of promising new platinum compounds, as well as drugs based on a chemical relative of platinum, *palladium*, which are effective against cancer but have fewer or milder side effects.

Another important group of chemicals used in cancer chemotherapy is the *antimetabolites*. These are chemicals that are very similar to *metabolites*—chemicals that the cell needs in order to live. If a cell takes in an antimetabolite, it is "fooled": Important cell enzymes combine with the antimetabolite instead of their normal metabolite and are held tightly. Then these enzymes cannot perform their normal tasks, and without them the cell cannot work properly. If enough of the antimetabolite is present, the cell may die. Some antimetabolites that are being used to treat cancer, especially leukemia, are *methotrexate*, *5-fluorouracil*, *6-mercaptopurine*, *arabinosylcytosine*, *thioguanine*, and *6-azauridine triacetate*. Methotrexate is very similar to the vitamin *folic acid* (one of the B vitamins). The other antimetabolites listed resemble the building blocks of nucleic acids; they prevent the growth of cancer cells by inhibiting the enzymes involved in DNA synthesis.

Another approach is to use a drug that destroys some

important chemical the cells need or interferes with some key step in its production. For example, certain kinds of cancer cells need a steady supply of an amino acid called *asparagine* in order to live and grow; but an enzyme normally found in the blood, called *L-asparaginase*, breaks down asparagine. *Hydroxyurea* is an anticancer chemical that blocks a key reaction in the production of one of the DNA building blocks, deoxycytidylic acid. And *procarbazine* probably acts as an alkylating agent and breaks up the DNA in the cell.

The search for chemical cures for cancer goes on. In an enormous testing program that spanned two decades, from 1955 to 1975, about 400,000 different compounds were screened for activity against cancer. Such a scattergun approach is no longer being used, as the emphasis in cancer research has shifted to other frontiers, but a number of new drugs are still being tested each year. Late in 1986, the National Cancer Institute (NCI) announced a major shift in drug-screening strategy. Instead of testing new drugs on mice with leukemia, NCI researchers now screen the drugs for activity against one hundred varieties of living cancer cells in laboratory dishes. The tests are highly automated; a scanning machine reads the results and feeds them to a computer, which analyzes the data. Promising compounds are then tested further in animals carrying the same strain of cancer. Researchers hope that the new system will select drugs that work better against the kinds of cancer found in most human patients.

People often wonder why it takes so long for a promising new drug to make its way from the laboratory to the front lines of medical practice. The answer is that every new drug must undergo a long and careful testing procedure, passing through several different stages. For cancer drugs, the first step is testing on cancer cells growing in a test tube or a culture dish. If a chemical kills such cancer cells or stops their growth, it progresses from this *in vitro* (literally meaning "in glass") stage to animal tests. Researchers can produce cancer in animals by transplanting cancer cells into their bodies, by treating them with carcinogens such as *benzpyrene*, or by infecting them with one of the viruses known to cause cancer in animals. There are also specially bred strains of mice that almost always develop cancer of a particular type at a particular age. If a drug is found to be effective in treating cancer in mice or rats, it may then be tested on larger animals such as dogs or monkeys. The most promising drugs graduate from animal tests to clinical trials on human cancer patients. These tests are carefully regulated, and generally the experiments provide for a group of *controls*, who receive either no treatment (if there is not an accepted treatment for the disease available) or the standard treatment used on patients in the general population. If a new drug seems to be as good as or better than the standard treatments, it is tested further on larger groups of patients. Meanwhile, careful tests are also conducted to determine whether the drug has any harmful side effects.

Finally, if the drug still seems promising, all the evidence is gathered and submitted to the Food and Drug Administration (FDA) for approval. With particularly deadly forms of cancer, researchers may be permitted to test drugs that have side effects, on the principle that the potential good of saving a patient's life far outweighs such harmful effects as vomiting (the toxic cancer drugs may damage cells in the delicate lining of the stomach and intestines), temporary loss of hair (due to damage to the hair follicles), or even more serious effects (doxorubicin, a valuable drug being used widely against breast cancer and soft-tissue sarcomas, can injure heart muscle). Sometimes new drugs are tested on *terminal* cancer patients (ones who seem surely doomed to die). Dramatic "miracle cures" have occasionally resulted, but tests on terminal cancer patients have also caused researchers to give up on drugs that were later found to be effective when used on patients with less advanced forms of the disease. The tests on terminal patients were disappointing merely because an advanced cancer produces such devastating effects on various body organs and systems that even a "miracle drug" could not save the patient. The FDA procedures for the licensing of a new drug can take years, but for especially promising and lifesaving drugs there are special "fast-track" shortcuts. In addition, a new drug may be made available on a "compassionate use" basis at doctors' request for patients who are not helped by any of the drugs that are already approved.

Anticancer chemicals have been found in plants from such far-off places as Brazil, China, and Madagascar. Skin divers searching the ocean bottoms have found some promising substances in clams and other sea creatures. Microbiologists working with molds and chemists synthesizing new chemicals in the laboratory have contributed many new candidates for anticancer drugs.

The cancer chemotherapist today has a wide assortment of drugs to call upon in the fight against cancer. But none of them is perfect. None of them is the "magic bullet" that cancer specialists dream of finding—the drug that will kill *only* cancer cells and leave normal body cells unharmed. Much of cancer research today is concentrated on searching for differences between cancer cells and normal cells. If such differences are found, scientists will be able to devise ways to take advantage of them to attack the cancer cells alone. Meanwhile, chemotherapists are working with the drugs they have and thinking up ingenious ways to make them safer and more effective.

For example, it was first thought that the enzyme L-asparaginase might be a "magic bullet" against leukemia. But, after researchers learned to produce large amounts of this rather complicated chemical, it was found that it did not work as well on people as it did in the original animal studies. Apparently, some of the normal cells, as well as the cancer cells, need asparagine; and large doses of the drug also kill these important normal cells. In addition, asparaginase is a protein, and usually obtained from bacteria that are grown in enormous numbers in huge tanks. The human body has a very effective system for recognizing the differences between its own proteins and those of other organisms. If any "foreign" proteins enter the blood, the body's disease-fighting cells attack them. So when asparaginase is injected into a leukemia patient, a furious battle begins. The foreign protein is destroyed. And, just as many innocent civilians may be killed or injured in a war, the body's fight against asparaginase can result in harm to important organs.

One clever way of getting around this difficulty is a technique called *microencapsulation*. Tiny droplets of a liquid containing asparaginase are enclosed inside a very thin membrane like a plastic bag. This membrane is a little like a sieve, for it contains many tiny openings. The particles (molecules) of asparaginase are too large to pass through the openings. But the amino acid asparagine is made up of much smaller molecules, which can move freely in and out of the microcapsules. Researchers at McGill University placed microcapsules of asparaginase in a solution of asparagine. Soon all the asparagine was broken down, even though all the asparaginase was safely locked inside the microcapsules. Then microcapsules with asparaginase were injected into mice. These mice and a group of untreated mice were then injected with tumor cells. The untreated mice all developed cancer, but many of the mice that received the microcapsules did not. Indeed, this treatment was much more effective than just injecting a solution of asparaginase, for the asparaginase held inside the microcapsules could break down the asparagine of the blood without provoking an attack by the body's defense system. After the successful animal tests, the microcapsule technique and related approaches were extended to humans.

In studies supported jointly by the National Institutes of Health (NIH) and a drug manufacturer, Enzon, Inc., a new technique for protecting asparaginase from the immune system is in the final stage of testing on children with *acute lymphoblastic leukemia* (ALL). The active enzyme is bonded to a waxy polymer substance, *polyethylene glycol*. The resulting drug, *PEG-L-asparaginase*, dissolves readily in salt solution or blood. After injection, it circulates in the bloodstream for an average of two weeks, compared to eighteen hours for the pure enzyme. It is not only less toxic than unmodified asparaginase, but it is more active: The effective dose of PEG-L-asparaginase is only one-hundredth of L-asparaginase alone. It is also cheaper and more effective than the microencapsulated drug.

One of the main problems in cancer chemotherapy is that a dose of a drug that is high enough to kill all the cancer cells may be so high that it damages too many normal cells, too. In addition, when there is a large, solid tumor, not all the cancer cells are in an actively growing and dividing state. Those on the outside of the tumor are, but the cancer cells buried deep within the tumor are in a sort of resting state.

So what often happens is that an anticancer drug simply kills the cells on the outside of the tumor. Then, when these cells are stripped away, the cells that are on the outside of the remaining tumor mass become active in turn. They begin to grow and divide wildly again, and the tumor grows—unless the patient is promptly given another dose of the drug. With enough doses, the tumor can gradually be killed, layer by layer, like peeling away the layers of an onion. But before the tumor is all gone, the drug may also have done serious damage to the rest of the body. In addition, when a drug is given over a long period of time, the cancer may build up a resistance to the drug. In any population of cells, there are some that are more sensitive to drugs than others. The sensitive cells are killed off first, but the cells that are less sensitive remain and can multiply. Eventually, resistant cells make up the whole population, and the drug is no longer effective against the cancer. (Cancers may develop resistance to radiation therapy in a similar way.) Researchers have figured out several ways around these problems.

First of all, *combined approaches* have now become the standard treatment for many types of cancer. Anticancer drugs are used together with surgery or radiation. After a surgeon has cut out a large, solid tumor, for example, chemotherapy can be used to "mop up," using small doses of drugs to kill off any stray cancer cells that remain or any tiny clumps of cancer cells that have migrated to other parts of the body. Many people who suspect they might have cancer put off going to the doctor because they are afraid that they will face a seriously disfiguring and perhaps even crippling operation. But when a surgeon knows that drugs and other treatments are available as a second line of attack, less tissue may be removed.

In the treatment of breast cancer, for example, for a long time the standard approach was an operation called a *radical mastectomy*—the removal not only of the tumor but also of the whole breast, the muscles under it, and the lymph nodes in the breast and underarm areas. In addition to the deep psychological adjustment that such surgery required, the operation often left the patient with some degree of pain and disability. Many women dreaded the "mutilation" of breast surgery so much that they refused to examine their breasts regularly, for fear of finding a lump. As a result, many cancers that could have been stopped if they had been caught early went undetected until they were so large they could no longer be ignored. By that time, the cancer was likely to have metastasized, and even a radical mastectomy could not save the woman's life. In recent years, however, a combination of new, more effective treatments and a strong consumer movement that encourages people to take a more active role in their medical treatments has prompted a reexamination of breast cancer treatment. Studies have shown that radical surgery gives no better results than *simple mastectomy* (removal only of the breast) or, in some cases, even *lumpectomy* (removal only of the cancerous lump), followed

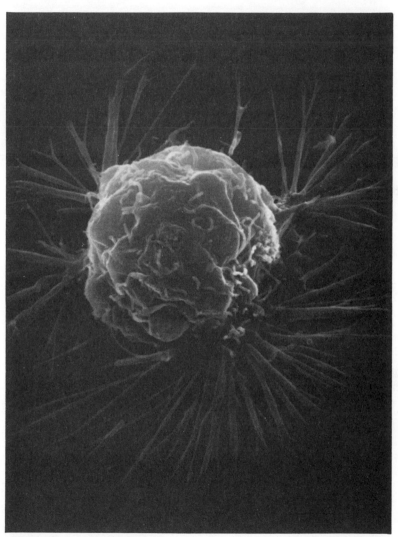

Scanning electron micrograph of a cell from human breast cancer tissue.

by chemotherapy and other treatments to kill off any remaining cancer cells. In a similar way, the combination of chemotherapy with surgery has made it possible to avoid amputating the limb in many bone cancers.

In addition to combinations of chemotherapy with surgery or radiation, oncologists also get around the harmful side effects of anticancer drugs by using *combinations of drugs* that work in different ways. Lower doses of each individual drug can be used, so that they all attack the cancer cells but do not harm the normal body cells very much. Early in 1976, the medical community and the general public were thrilled by the report of an Italian study, supported by the American National Cancer Institute, on the treatment of breast cancer with a combination of drugs after radical mastectomy. The drug combination CMF (cyclophosphamide, methotrexate, and 5-fluorouracil) produced a much better survival rate, free of recurrences of cancer, than surgery alone. The study was hailed as a work "of monumental importance," not only because the new technique would save the lives of thousands of women with breast cancer each year, but also because similar approaches could be applied to other cancers as well.

The Italian studies, reported by Gianni Bonadonna, were later confirmed by follow-up studies of the same group of women, as well as the results of treatment of other groups of patients with breast cancer, bone cancer, a form of lung cancer, and a variety of others. Studies of combination chemotherapy for Hodgkin's disease, a deadly cancer of the lymph nodes, were begun at the National Cancer Institute in 1964. At that time, fewer than 10 percent of Hodgkin's disease patients survived more than five years with the usual treatments. But combination chemotherapy produced complete remission in 80 percent of the patients studied. A follow-up study in 1976 found that two thirds of these patients had not suffered relapses; many of them are still alive and cancer free today. Combination chemotherapy transformed Hodgkin's disease from one of the most deadly cancers to one of the most curable. Drug combinations have worked similar wonders with leukemia patients.

Researchers are still studying the effects of the various anticancer drugs and their combinations, trying to work out such details as whether it is better to give several drugs at once or one after another, and in what order. Studies have shown, for example, that if methotrexate is given before 5-fluorouracil, the 5-fluorouracil is more effective. Other studies have revealed that cancer cells are more sensitive to the action of drugs at certain times of day. National Cancer Institute researchers are discovering characteristic proteins that can identify drug-resistant cancer cells. An approach called *front loading* gives the most effective drugs first in order to knock out cancer cells that might have become resistant if weaker drugs had been used. Another ingenious approach is the *drug rescue* technique. Dramatic results have been obtained in lymphosarcoma; cancer of the breast, lung, pancreas, and uterus; as well as melanoma, neuroblastoma (a nerve cancer), and various bone cancers. The patient is first given a high dose of the antimetabolite methotrexate. High doses of this drug knock out cancer cells very effectively, but they also can kill normal cells. So twelve hours later, the patients are given another drug called *citrovorum factor*, which acts as an antidote to methotrexate. The first drug kills the cancer cells, and the second one rescues the patients. (This was the treatment used for Edward Kennedy, Jr., who had a type of bone cancer.)

According to recent studies at Colorado State University, the drug *verapamil* can reverse cancer cells' drug resistance. Verapamil, which belongs to a group of drugs called *calcium channel blockers* that regulate the flow of chemicals through cell membranes, is already being used widely to treat heart disorders and migraine headaches. In experiments on dogs with tumors, the Colorado researchers found that verapamil, administered late in a course of treatment when the cancer cells have developed resistance to anticancer drugs, makes the cells vulnerable to the drugs again. The researchers are currently conducting further studies to determine whether administering verapamil at the beginning of chemotherapy can prevent drug resistance from developing at all.

Photodynamic therapy is another way of making chemotherapy more effective and less damaging to normal cells. First a harmless drug that makes tumor cells light sensitive is injected, and then the tumors are exposed to light. The combination seems especially promising for destroying lung, skin, eye, and bladder cancers. In another variation, called *extracorporeal photopheresis*, patients with a rare form of leukemia in which abnormal white blood cells accumulate in the skin are given a drug called 8-*methoxypsoralen* (8-MOP), a natural substance found in vegetables and fruits such as limes and figs. Then the patient is hooked up to a machine that removes the white blood cells from the blood and returns the rest of the blood to the body. For four hours, the white cells circulate through clear plastic tubing, 1 millimeter thick, where they are exposed to more 8-MOP and ultraviolet light. The light activates 8-MOP, which homes in on cells that are dividing actively—such as the abnormal cancer cells. The activated drug acts on the cell's DNA, binding its two strands tightly together so that it cannot replicate. Some of the cells are killed outright, and others are damaged. When they are returned to the body, they turn the body's own defenses—the immune system—back on and stimulate the body to fight the cancer.

Another approach that is being used more widely is *hyperthermia*, the use of heat to kill tumor cells or make them more sensitive to drugs, radiations, or immunotherapy. The idea is an old one. Back in 1866, a German doctor reported that a facial tumor in one of his patients disappeared spontaneously after the patient came down with a streptococcal infection that produced a high fever. A few years later, William Coley, a New York surgeon, noticed a similar "miracle cure": A man with terminal sarcoma recovered completely after suffering a high fever from an infection. The doctor developed fever-producing bacterial injections, and some of his cancer patients lived on for fifty years after they had seemed to be doomed to death. The dramatic results may have been due more to a stimulation of the body's immune defenses than to the heat of the fever. At any rate, the bacterial injections were themselves very dangerous, and the technique was abandoned. In a study in the mid-1960's, researchers were able to shrink the tumors of six out of twenty-two cancer patients by heating their blood to over 41.5° C (106.7° F). The idea of hyperthermia did not really take off, however, until the mid-1970's, when a number of research groups used radio waves or microwaves, transmitted through a tiny antenna implanted in the tumor, to heat up the cancer cells. (Other groups have used ultrasound or magnetic induction to produce the heating effect, reaching temperatures as high as 50° C [122° F] in the tumors.) A number of theories have been suggested to explain why heat kills tumor cells or makes them more sensitive to drugs and other treatments, while leaving normal tissues unharmed. First of all, the circulation around tumors is usually rather poor, and thus they tend to concentrate heat, whereas it is carried away from normal tissues by the blood flowing through them. The low levels of oxygen and nutrients and the rather acid conditions in tumor cells, in comparison with normal cells, may make them more vulnerable to heat. The heat may also cause the breakdown of proteins in the tumor cell membranes.

The recent history of cancer research and treatment has shown a clear trend toward combined approaches—combinations of drugs, combinations of drugs with surgery or radiation treatment, combinations of heat with drugs or radiations, and so forth. Some of the most hopeful results are coming from combinations of these treatments with immunological approaches, using the body's own defenses to fight cancer or using special products of the immune defenses called *monoclonal antibodies*. These are complicated chemicals that react very specifically with a particular chemical—perhaps a chemical found on the surface of cancer cells. Specially tailored monoclonals can be used to devise sensitive tests for cancer, picking up the telltale traces of malignant cells when the tumors are too small to be detected by any other means. They can also be used, both by themselves and in combination with drugs or radioisotopes, to home in on cancer cells and kill them selectively. Many researchers believe that in monoclonal antibodies they may finally have found the "magic bullets" against cancer for which they have been searching for so many years. These exciting new weapons in the fight against cancer will be discussed in the next chapter.

6. Helping the Body to Help Itself

At this very moment you are under attack. Invisible invaders—billions of them—are lurking, waiting for the slightest gap in your defenses. Hidden in the harmless-seeming things around you (even in the food you eat and the air you breathe) and swarming on your skin, they will take every opportunity to slip inside your body. And there, in your blood and tissues, fierce battles are raging. Invading bacteria and viruses are being challenged by your body's defenders. White blood cells are attacking bacteria and gobbling them up. Viruses are being dealt with by fast-acting *interferons*, a family of proteins that keep them from multiplying too rapidly. Proteins called *antibodies* also help in the fight.

These are the body's normal defenses against infectious diseases—diseases caused by bacteria, viruses, and other microbes. The antibodies provide long-lasting protection from disease germs. The body has a sort of chemical sense, with which it recognizes all the tens of thousands of its own chemical substances. If a "foreign" chemical, or *antigen*, penetrates into the body, a series of reactions begins. Certain cells of the body's defense system build up antibodies that fit the foreign antigen perfectly, attacking only that chemical and targeting it for attack by blood proteins or specialized white blood cells. After the antigen has disappeared from the body, some samples of the specific antibody-producing cells are kept on hand. Then, if the body is invaded by this antigen again, large supplies of the specific antibodies that match it can be produced quickly.

The body can make antibodies against the chemicals that form the outer coats of bacteria and viruses. Once a supply of antibodies against a particular disease germ is on hand, the person is said to be *immune* to that disease. The body can also make antibodies against various other complicated chemicals that happen to get into the bloodstream or tissues. Sometimes this system works too well, and the person develops an *allergy* to some food or the pollen of a plant. The body reacts to this harmless chemical as though it were a deadly microbe.

The body's disease fighters are the white blood cells. Some white blood cells gobble up invading microbes, actually eating them. *Macrophages* are an important kind of this type of white blood cell. Their name literally means "big eaters." Other white blood cells, the *lymphocytes*, are involved in the immunity mechanisms—recognizing the differences between the body's own cells and "foreigners" and providing the patterns for antibodies against invaders. The name of these cells means "lymph cells," and they are often to be found in the various lymph nodes scattered through the body (for example, in the neck and under the arms) and traveling through the system of lymph vessels, as well as in the bloodstream and the spleen.

Immunologists have discovered two important kinds of lymphocytes: *B cells* and *T cells*. B cells are formed in the bone marrow and produce antibodies. The T cells are also formed in the bone marrow but mature in the thymus gland; they have many important tasks in protecting the body. T cells act as the body's watchdogs. They constantly patrol the body, moving through the blood and lymph circulations and even slipping between cells to rove through tissues. It is the T cells' job to recognize the body's own cells and to alert the body's defenses against foreign chemicals. Specialized T cells can act as killers, attacking virus-infected cells and some tumor cells. Like antibodies, these killer T cells recognize specific antigens. Another type—*helper T cells*—help B cells to make antibodies; still others, *suppressor T cells*,

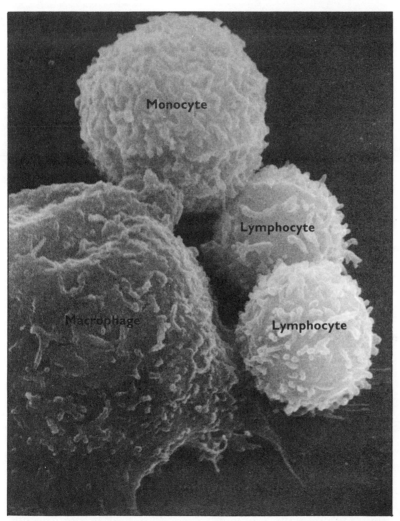

Scanning electron micrograph of the body's white cell defenders: a macrophage, a monocyte, and two lymphocytes.

stop the B cells from becoming active. T cells also make chemical messengers called *lymphokines*, some of which can make macrophages gather around and swell up to become active, "angry" germ eaters. In addition to the macrophages, B cells, and T cells, the body's white cell defenders include a type called *natural killers*, or *NK cells*. They attack abnormal cells such as tumor cells or virus-infected cells, but they are not as specific as the killer T cells.

Many researchers believe that one of the main jobs of the T cells is *immune surveillance*—keeping watch over the body to make sure that none of its cells has changed and become foreign. It is thought that cells are continually—perhaps even every day—changing into cancer cells. But when they change, they become different enough for T cells to recognize the difference and attack them. So the tiny cancers are killed off before they have a chance to grow very much. But sometimes the immune surveillance slips up or is unable to handle the growing tumor cells. Some cancer researchers believe that the different parts of the immune system may sometimes even interfere with each other. B cells may get sensitized to tumor cells and produce antibodies against them—but then the antibodies, instead of killing the cancer cells, shield them so that the T cells cannot get to them. Or growing cancer cells may shed antigens into the tissues surrounding them. When these cancer antigens get into the circulation, they may combine with anticancer antibodies in the blood, tying them up so that they do not work against the actual cancer cells.

There is some good evidence for these theories. For example, surgeons have been perfecting methods of transplanting organs such as kidneys and even hearts into people whose own organs are badly damaged. Normally, the body would recognize that the transplanted organ contains many foreign chemicals and would make antibodies against them. Soon the transplant would shrivel up and die. This process is called *rejection*. Transplant surgeons are therefore using drugs or radiation to temporarily knock out the body's immune system. By the time it recovers and begins to make antibodies again, the transplanted organ has been a part of the body for so long that it may not seem foreign anymore. In this way, it can be saved from rejection.

In using antirejection treatments, doctors have to be very careful to protect transplant patients from infections. Without their usual defenses, these patients are very susceptible to infections that a normal person could fight off easily. Even a common cold could threaten a transplant patient's life. It has been discovered that transplant patients also have a much higher than normal chance of developing malignant tumors. This finding supports the idea that the immune system helps to protect people from cancer. Further support is provided by studies of *AIDS* (acquired immune deficiency syndrome), a disease in which a retrovirus attacks helper T cells, growing in them and ultimately killing them. Without this key part of the immune system, AIDS patients' immune defenses are severely depressed. The patients not only come down with a number of *opportunistic infections*—rare bacterial, viral, fungal, and parasitic diseases that people with a normal immune system do not usually catch—but they are also prone to develop a type of cancer called *Kaposi's sarcoma* (KS). People with KS have large, purplish marks on their skin, which look like bruises but are not painful. AIDS first appeared in the United States in the late 1970's. Before then, KS was a very rare type of cancer in the U.S., seen mainly in old men, and it was a rather mild, slow-growing cancer. But in AIDS patients, whose immune system has been damaged by the disease, KS spreads quickly, attacking organs and glands of the body and killing within months. AIDS patients may also develop lymphomas of the central nervous system.

The idea that the immune system is involved in cancer points the way to a whole new approach to devising tests for cancer and developing possible cures. Researchers have been searching for specific cancer antigens that could be used as the basis of tests to recognize the presence of cancer cells and perhaps to target them for more effective attack by drugs. Some of the typical cancer-cell antigens that have been found, such as *carcinoembryonic antigen* (CEA) and *alpha-fetoprotein* (AFP), have proved to be too general to be used in reliable cancer tests: They are found not only on cancer cells, but also on some types of normal cells. Other cancer antigens have proved to be very narrowly specific for particular types of cancer. But Boston University researcher Samuel Bogoch and his colleagues have discovered a family of more general cancer antigens, the *recognins*, which seem to be characteristic of the process of malignant transformation.

The recognins are a group of small proteins, all chemically very similar to one another. Interestingly enough, a computer search through all the known protein structures revealed that the recognins are related to some enzymes of

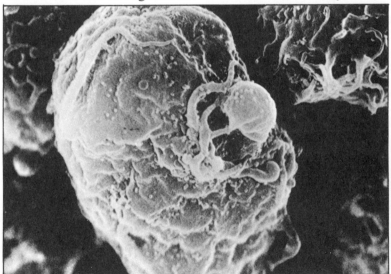

Scanning electron micrograph of a helper T cell infected with AIDS (HIV) virus. The virus can be seen budding from the cell membrane of the T cell.

cell respiration. Scientists call these enzymes *anaerobic* because they work in the absence of air. Cancer cells rely on anaerobic respiration to generate the energy they need for their furious growth, whereas normal cells use oxygen in respiration. This is one of the important differences between cancer cells and normal cells.

The first two recognins, *astrocytin* and *malignin*, were found in a brain tumor, but the Bogoch team soon discovered malignin like antigens in a variety of other types of tumors. What is more, they found that when a cancer is growing actively, the body produces *antimalignin*—antibodies against malignin. The blood of healthy, cancer-free people contains a small amount of antimalignin, too; it is apparently a part of the normal immune surveillance. In the presence of cancer, however, the antimalignin levels rise sharply. Gradually, if the tumor becomes established and the body begins to lose its fight against it, an increasing fraction of the antimalignin in the blood is partly broken down into fragments. Bogoch believes that the ability to break down antimalignin antibodies is one of the defenses cancer cells can develop against the body's attacks. Eventually, in terminal cancer patients, the antimalignin level in the blood falls.

The Bogoch team has developed a method for determining antimalignin levels in blood samples, which became widely available for clinical use in mid-1987. Judging by more than 3,000 double-blind tests of blood sera from cancer patients and normal blood donors, the antimalignin method gives no false negatives (cases in which the test fails to show a cancer that is present), except for terminal patients, and a very low level of false positives (cases in which the test gives a positive reading when there actually is no cancer present). There are only 6 percent false positives, which drops to 0.4 percent when the test is repeated. (CEA tests, in contrast, usually give at least 10 to 15 percent false positives.) The antimalignin test will not be useful for general screening of the population, since it indicates only that an active cancer is present but gives no clues to what kind it might be or where it might be located. However, it should be an invaluable aid in cases in which cancer is suspected but other tests have failed to detect it—or the alternative tests are painful and dangerous. It may also be useful for periodically testing people in special cancer-risk groups—for example, women with close relatives who have had breast cancer.

Meanwhile, other research teams are working on immunological approaches to the treatment of cancer. They are seeking ways to strengthen the patient's immune system and help it to recognize cancer cells as foreign so that the body itself can fight off the cancer more effectively. Some doctors are testing drugs that stimulate the immune system. Such substances have been obtained from bacteria and yeasts, from the livers of sharks, and even from the tissues of people and animals with cancer.

One immune stimulator that has received a great deal of attention from cancer researchers is *BCG*. This is a live-bacteria vaccine that has been used in Europe for many years to protect people against tuberculosis. In addition to stimulating the formation of antibodies against tuberculosis bacilli, BCG seems to activate the body's immune system against cancer cells. When BCG is injected into a tumor or applied on scratches made in the tumor's surface, macrophages move into the area and begin to attack the cancer cells. In some cases, the tumors disappear completely.

Another immune stimulator was discovered by a lucky accident. A French veterinarian was trying to develop a vaccine for a livestock disease, brucellosis. He produced a vaccine that protected his experimental cattle from the disease, but other researchers using the same vaccine were unable to duplicate his results. Trying to figure out why, the researcher had a flash of insight. Before the vaccination, his cattle had been wormed with an antiworm drug, *levamisole*. Perhaps that drug was somehow making the vaccine more effective. Follow-up experiments revealed that levamisole may help to stimulate the immune system, making it more responsive to antigens.

Levamisole, like BCG, has given positive results in tests on animal cancers and has helped to increase the survival rate of some human cancer patients. But both of these immune stimulators have drawbacks, and unresolved problems still remain. Some patients, for example, become allergic to BCG and may suffer from unpleasant or even dangerous side effects. *Freund's adjuvant*, another immune stimulator, also has its drawbacks: A sore develops at the site of the injection and takes a long time to heal; the scab may remain for more than a year. Levamisole lacks those disadvantages, but, like the other two, it does not always produce clear-cut results. In some cases, patients who received immune stimulators after surgery, radiation treatment, or chemotherapy had a better chance to survive than the controls, who received only the conventional treatments. But in other clinical trials, patients who received immune stimulators had a poorer survival rate than the controls! In general, immune stimulators work best when the bulk of the tumor has been removed by surgery or killed off by radiation or chemotherapy, and only a few tumor cells remain to be mopped up.

Some cancer researchers have been obtaining promising results by combining immune stimulators with vaccines tailor-made against the patient's own cancer. One of the pioneering studies was reported in 1976 by researchers from the University of Ottawa. Forty-one patients with lung cancer were treated by surgery to remove their tumors. Then the patients were divided into four groups. One group received no further treatment, the second group received chemotherapy (methotrexate with citrovorum rescue), the third group was given immunotherapy, and the fourth group received a combination of chemotherapy and immunotherapy. For the immunotherapy, the patients' tumors were sent to Ariel Hollinshead at George Washington University in Washington, D.C. She prepared a vaccine from each tumor and then airmailed it back to Ottawa. The patients received the vaccine in combination with the immune stimulator Freund's adjuvant. All twenty-six patients who received immunotherapy, either with or without chemotherapy, were still alive after periods of up to three years and were found to be making antibodies against their cancer antigens. Later follow-up studies of these patients revealed that 78 percent of the patients who received immunotherapy were still alive after five years, compared with a five-year survival rate of only 46 percent among the controls. Hollinshead and her associates are currently working on vaccines for colon, ovarian, and skin cancers. In another study, reported in 1984 by Michael G. Hanna, Jr., of the Litton Institute of Applied Biotechnology, BCG combined with a vaccine against the patients' own tumors reduced the death rate in a group of forty colon cancer patients by two thirds in comparison with conventional treatments. In general, however, researchers have found it very difficult to immunize cancer patients against their own tumors.

Some of the most exciting immune stimulators now being studied by cancer researchers are natural body substances: interferon, a substance called tumor necrosis factor, and a lymphokine called interleukin-2.

Interferon is the biological agent that has been known for the longest time. It was first discovered in 1957 by Alick Isaacs and Jean Lindenmann, working at the National Institute of Medical Research in London. They found that cells

HOW INTERFERON WORKS

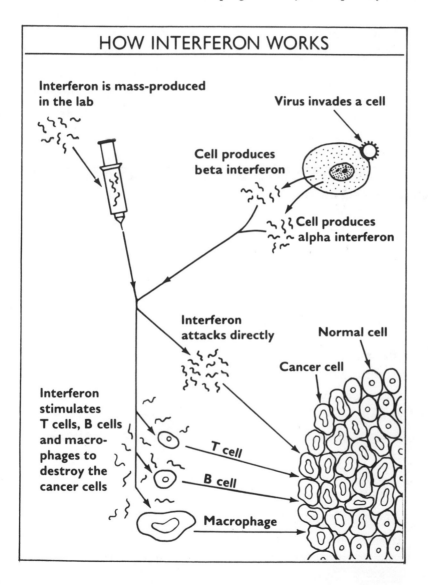

Interferon is mass-produced
in the lab

Virus invades a cell

Cell produces
beta interferon

Cell produces
alpha interferon

Interferon
attacks directly

Normal cell

Cancer cell

Interferon
stimulates
T cells, B cells
and macro-
phages to
destroy the
cancer cells

T cell

B cell

Macrophage

of chick embryos infected with influenza virus released a substance that could be added to other cells to make them resistant to the flu virus. In the years that followed, researchers found that this substance, interferon, is a protein that is released from cells infected by viruses and prevents viruses from reproducing. It does not protect the original infected cell, but it does protect other cells, thus helping to keep the virus from spreading. Interferon works not only against the original virus that stimulated its production but against other viruses, too, and it is also effective against tumor cells. In addition to its direct effects, interferon can work with various parts of the immune system, increasing or decreasing antibody production by B cells, boosting the secretion of lymphokines by T cells, and activating killer T cells, natural killers, and macrophages.

For a long time, interferon research was held back by the fact that interferon is produced in extremely tiny amounts, so that it was difficult to get enough of it to purify and study. It was also virtually impossible to get enough to use for treating people, because this protein does not work across species lines: Chick or cattle or pig interferon does not work on humans; only human interferon is effective in human patients. In addition, even within a single species, interferon proved to be not a single protein but a whole family of proteins. Virus-infected cells, for example, produce two main types, α- and β-interferons, and stimulated lymphocytes secrete γ-interferon, which acts as a lymphokine.

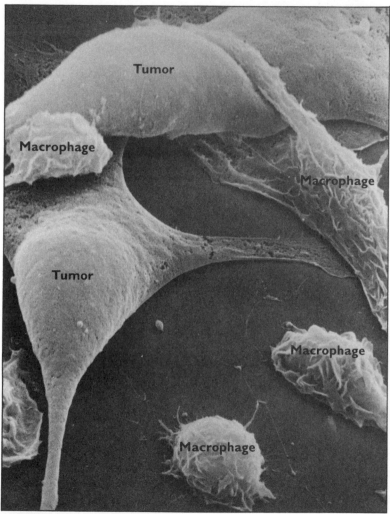

Scanning electron micrograph of activated mouse macrophages attacking mouse melanoma tumors. The macrophages will kill the tumor cells.

The picture changed dramatically in the early 1980's, when *recombinant DNA* techniques were developed and applied on an industrial scale. Today's biotechnologists are able to take genes from any organism—even humans—and insert them into microorganisms such as bacteria. (The common intestinal bacterium *Escherichia coli* has been a favorite in recombinant DNA work.) Ways have been developed to multiply the inserted genes into hundreds or even thousands of copies and to turn them on so that they direct the production of proteins. You might not think that a microscopic bacterium could produce a significant amount of protein, but microbiologists can now grow bacteria in tanks. So bacteria can be used as miniature factories for producing substances such as interferon—not in the minute fractions of a gram that scientists previously had to work with, but in pounds. Tests show that recombinant DNA interferons are identical with the natural proteins produced in virus-infected human cells.

The first results of interferon tests on cancer patients were rather disappointing, mainly because the protein was used on patients with very advanced cancers who were too far gone to be helped. But later studies have been more promising. Interferon has been found to be very effective in treating certain myelomas and lymphomas and the chronic phase of chronic myelogenous leukemia (CML); studies of its action on other forms of cancer are under way. Combinations

EFFECTS OF TUMOR NECROSIS FACTOR ON CELLS GROWN IN CULTURE.

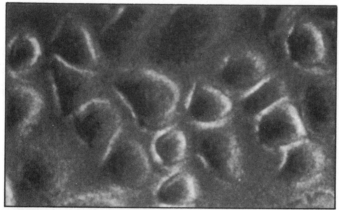

Live, human cervical cells grown in the laboratory.

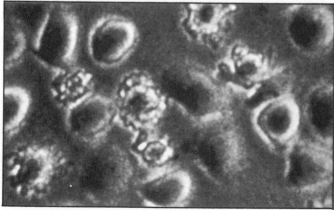

24 hours after treatment with TNF: the cell walls are disrupted and the cells' internal contents are released, resulting in cell death.

of interferon with chemotherapy seem particularly promising.

Another natural anticancer substance, *tumor necrosis factor* (TNF), is part of the body's normal response to infection. It is produced by macrophages stimulated by a bacterial infection. Tumor necrosis factor may act as a growth factor for some normal cells, but it is toxic for other types, especially the endothelial cells that line the blood vessels. It is also toxic for many cancer cells, stopping them from growing or even destroying them. Thus, TNF can make tumors shrink, promoting their *resorption* by the body. It has been found that TNF fits perfectly into special chemical receptors on the surface of cells, combining with them in a reaction very similar to the reaction of an antibody to its specific antigen. First discovered in 1971 by Lloyd Old at the Memorial Sloan-Kettering Cancer Center in New York, TNF received a tremendous boost from the development of biotechnology. Now available in large amounts, it has successfully passed the test-tube and animal stages of research and is being tested on human cancer patients.

There are some reservations aginst the use of TNF as an anticancer agent, however. Researchers led by Anthony Cerami at Rockefeller University have found that TNF is identical to *cachectin*, a cell product that causes *cachexia* (wasting away) in people with chronic bacterial and parasitic diseases, as well as in cancer patients. This same substance is involved in the severe shock produced by some bacterial toxins—a condition that is often lethal. Tumor necrosis factor also can cause fever and increased blood clotting, and it stimulates the release of factors that cause pain and destruction of the joints. With all these powerful biological effects, TNF is a substance to be used with caution, and in as small amounts as possible. One approach that seems promising is its use in combination with interferon: TNF makes interferon more effective against both viruses and cancer.

One of the newest and most promising biological agents is *interleukin-2*. This is a lymphokine that stimulates some of the T lymphocytes to develop into killer T cells, able to attack and kill invading microbes and cancer cells. In December 1985, the results of a National Cancer Institute study of interleukin-2 on advanced cancer patients were published in the prestigious *New England Journal of Medicine*. In an approach known as *adoptive immunotherapy*, white blood cells were removed from the patients' bodies, treated with interleukin-2 to stimulate the formation of killer T cells, and then these *lymphokine-activated killer* (LAK) cells were reinjected into the patients' bloodstreams. In eleven out of twenty-five patients, with such cancers as a rectal cancer that had spread to the lungs, kidney cancer that had produced metastatic lung tumors, and various metastatic melanomas, the tumors were reduced in size by more than 50 percent. In one case, the cancer disappeared completely. The press publicized the report with headlines suggesting that a cancer cure had finally been found. Thousands of frantic cancer patients

HOW INTERLEUKIN-2 WORKS IN ADOPTIVE IMMUNOTHERAPY

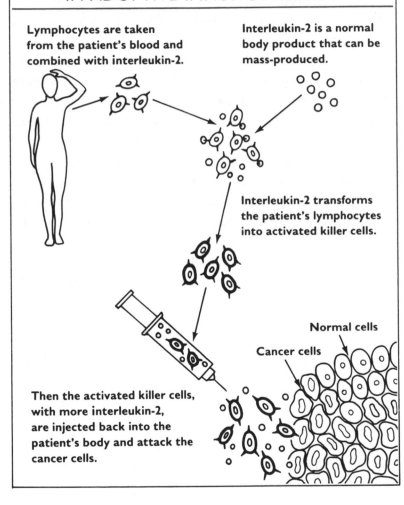

Lymphocytes are taken from the patient's blood and combined with interleukin-2.

Interleukin-2 is a normal body product that can be mass-produced.

Interleukin-2 transforms the patient's lymphocytes into activated killer cells.

Normal cells

Cancer cells

Then the activated killer cells, with more interleukin-2, are injected back into the patient's body and attack the cancer cells.

phoned the National Cancer Institute and the American Cancer Society, asking how they could obtain the new treatment.

Steven Rosenberg, the head of the research team, hastened to explain that the new technique, though very promising, was still experimental. The interleukin-2 approach is a very complicated procedure, and there are serious side effects. Fluid retention can result in weight gains of 10 percent, and in some patients fluid accumulated in the lungs, producing severe breathing difficulties. Chills and fevers also developed after the injection of LAK cells. These side effects were so serious that the patients had to be hospitalized during the treatments.

Preliminary results from the LAK experiments were promising, but a larger study showed that the treatments were less effective and much more toxic than had originally been thought. Rosenberg's team has tried a new approach, using T cells isolated from the tumor and thus increasing the proportions of cells that specifically recognize tumor antigens. Treating these cells with interleukin-2 and reintroducing them into the patient has yielded promising preliminary results.

A 1987 follow-up report evaluating the results of the adoptive immunotherapy approach revealed that 29 out of 152 patients treated either with interleukin-2 alone or with LAK cells had complete or partial remissions that improved their condition and prolonged their lives. One woman with melanoma was still free of any signs of cancer more than two years after the treatment. Other patients showed mild favorable responses, but for the majority there was no improvement, and four patients died as a result of effects of the treatment.

Meanwhile, a team at Huntington Medical Research Institutes in Pasadena, California, is using a similar approach to treat patients with malignant brain tumors. These tumors, which usually kill within a year of diagnosis, are being removed surgically. Then interleukin-2-stimulated white blood cells are placed directly into the hole in the brain left by the removal of the tumor. Patients who had failed to respond to the usual treatments and had a life expectancy of only three months showed improvement after the experimental immunotherapy; nine out of nineteen treated were still alive after more than a year, and those who died had survived for an average of thirty-eight weeks, nearly three times as long as expected. Research on interleukin-2 and other aspects of the natural immune mechanisms is continuing. The biotechnology firm Cetus is tinkering with the interleukin-2 molecule, changing an amino acid here or there and observing the effects. At least one of the changes already tried makes the anticancer action more effective. Cetus is also testing TNF, as well as one of the forms of human interferon, and another group of natural substances called *colony-stimulating factors* (CSF). Various forms of CSF work on the bone marrow to stimulate the production of white blood cells such as granulocytes and macrophages, and can cause some leukemic cells to differentiate. National Cancer Institute researcher Steven Rosenberg believes that colony-stimulating factors may be effective for cancer patients who do not respond to interleukin-2, and is currently studying these biological agents. Sloan-Kettering researchers used a form of CSF to restore the damaged bone marrow of cancer patients receiving chemotherapy. One of the most damaging side effects of many anticancer drugs is their severe destruction of bone marrow cells, and thus a combination with CSF can make chemotherapy more effective.

Another biotechnology firm, Immunex, is working exclusively on studies of lymphokines. One current line of investigation is directed at the factors that make B cells multiply, which may yield yet another generation of disease fighters.

Other groups of researchers are working on ways to activate macrophages so that they will attack and kill cancer cells. These roving scavengers could hunt down tiny metastases, too small to be detected, and destroy them before they grow into dangerous tumors. At M. D. Anderson Tumor Hospital and Tumor Institute in Houston, Isaiah Fidler has packaged the macrophage activators gamma-interferon and muramyl tripeptide into tiny *liposomes*. A thin ribbon of lipoprotein similar to the ones found in cell membranes is wound into a microscopic role, with the macrophage activators sandwiched between the lipoprotein layers. When such liposomes are injected into the bloodstream, macrophages gobble them up and digest them, which releases the activators. Injections of the liposomes saved 75 percent of mice with malignant melanoma that had metastasized to the lymph nodes and lungs. Similar results have been obtained in experiments with dogs at the University of Wisconsin.

Still another natural substance from the body's immune system is being enlisted in the fight against cancer. This is *thymosin*, a hormone produced by the thymus gland. Thymosin is believed to be the substance that activates T cells and makes them able to recognize the difference between the body's own cells and foreign antigens. As people get older, their thymus glands normally shrink, and at the same time, their immune systems grow less efficient. Injections of thymosin might help to rejuvenate the immune system, making it a more effective guard against both infectious diseases and cancer. Like many other natural body chemicals, thymosin is normally produced in very small amounts. But researchers have been able to isolate the genes involved in the production of human thymosin and to make large quantities of the protein by recombinant DNA methods. Now this hormone is being tested on cancer patients.

There is growing evidence that the foods we eat have a great influence on the workings of the immune system, and that certain vitamins, minerals, and other food chemicals can help to stimulate a flagging immune system.

Nobel Prize winner Linus Pauling, who started a controversy that is still raging when he proposed that taking large amounts of *vitamin C* can prevent the common cold, entered the cancer field in the mid-1970's. In 1976, Pauling and Ewan

Cameron, a Scottish medical researcher, announced the results of a study of one hundred terminal cancer patients.
These dying patients, who had not been helped by any of
the usual treatments, were given doses of 10 grams of vitamin
C a day. (This is a very large dose—a "megadose"—far
larger than a person would normally consume in foods.)
Compared with one hundred other terminal cancer patients
who had been treated at the same hospital without receiving
vitamin C, the vitamin-treated patients showed a dramatic
difference. They survived longer—three to twenty times as
long as the control patients; and eighteen of the vitamin-
treated patients were still alive at the time of the study, long
after they would have been expected to die. The researchers
speculated that vitamin C may help cells to produce an in-
hibitor that stops the action of the enzyme *hyaluronidase*.
This enzyme is produced in large amounts by cancer cells
and assists in breaking down the thick "ground substance"
found in the spaces between cells that may help to keep
normal cells in check. By stopping the action of hyaluronidase, Pauling and Cameron suggested, vitamin C may check
the spread of the cancer. In addition, the vitamin is known
to strengthen the immune system and the natural hormone
defenses that help the body to resist cancer.

Many medical experts objected that Pauling and Cameron's experiments were not well enough designed, and some
report they were unable to repeat the dramatic results. But
they do not dispute the value of vitamin C—at least in the

lower doses found in foods—in stimulating the immune system and possibly providing some protection against developing cancer. The same is true of some other important nutrients.

Vitamin A is another of the natural cancer fighters found in foods. It has been known since 1925 that when animals are fed a diet lacking in vitamin A, cells in their skin and mucous membranes begin to divide and multiply abnormally. These cells begin to look very much like precancerous cells—changed cells that might develop into cancer. For many years, little was done to follow up this finding. But then experiments showed that when vitamin A is given together with BCG, an immune stimulator, the combination is one hundred times as effective as BCG alone in fighting actively growing cancers. There is a problem with using vitamin A as an anticancer drug, though. In small doses, the vitamin is necessary for good health. But in large doses (more than people normally receive in food or in the standard multivitamin supplements), vitamin A can cause liver damage. The doses recommended for anticancer treatment are ten to one hundred times the levels normally considered toxic.

National Cancer Institute researchers turned to synthetic vitamin A derivatives, chemically modified forms called *retinoids*, which can be used in much higher doses without the harmful effects on the liver. In experiments on small animals, such as mice, rats, and hamsters, treated with powerful carcinogens, retinoids were found to cause precancerous cells to turn back into normal cells, thus preventing the development of cancer. Synthetic retinoids are now being given to people in high-risk groups, such as women who have had surgery for breast cancer or persons who have had lung cancer removed. (Their bodies might be expected to contain precancerous cells, and the retinoids can help to prevent recurrence of cancer.) Promising results have also been obtained in the treatment of skin and bladder cancers.

Another immune-stimulating vitamin is *vitamin E*. This is a natural antioxidant that can prevent the formation of highly reactive oxidized forms of natural body chemicals, which many researchers believe may play a role in the changes leading to cancer. It thus may provide some protection against developing cancer, although it is not generally effective in treating cancer patients. Vitamin E is helped in its action in the body by a mineral called *selenium*. This mineral plays a key role in maintaining a healthy and effective immune system. An easy way to remember these important nutrients is to think of them as "ACES," for the first letters of the vitamins A, C, and E and the mineral selenium. Another mineral that may be important in the body's defenses against cancer is *zinc*. This element is a part of many key enzymes in the body. It is important in the healing of cuts and sores, and it helps in the work of the immune system.

One of the most intriguing and controversial areas of immunology research today is a new subdivision called *psychoneuroimmunology*. There is a growing amount of evidence to indicate that a person's mental and emotional state can produce actual physical effects on the immune system and help to determine how well he or she can fight disease— including cancer. Studies of this brain-body connection have shown that the microbe-fighting white blood cells are more active when a person is in love, whereas stress has a variety of upsetting effects on the body, including a suppression of the responses of the white blood cells. The death of a spouse or some other close family member, the loss of a job, and other high-stress experiences can make people more vulnerable to cancer and other diseases. Yet stress is not always bad for the body; in fact, sometimes it acts to tone up the body and strengthen its defenses. The key seems to be a sense of being able to control the situation, or a feeling of hope. In one study, young rats that were taught to stop or avoid a stressful electric shock by pressing a lever were much less likely to develop cancer in later life than rats who received similar shocks but had no way to avoid them.

Some studies have shown that cancer patients with an active, positive outlook stand a better chance to survive than those who passively accept their condition with feelings of hopelessness. The best survival rates were observed among those with a fighting spirit, with the attitude "I'm going to conquer this thing."

Several recently reported studies suggest that emotional support, provided by close ties with family or friends, can also have a positive effect on survival from cancer and other illnesses. In a ten-year study of twenty-seven hundred people in a small Michigan town, those who led lonely lives, with few close personal relationships and little participation in group activities, had an overall death rate four times as high as those whose life-styles were more sociable. In another project, researchers followed nearly seven thousand residents of Alameda County, California, for seventeen years. They found that social isolation—defined as having few close friends and relatives and feeling alone even when friends are present—seemed to increase the risk of dying from cancer. Women who were socially isolated at the beginning of the study were twice as likely to contract cancers and three times as likely to die from them as more sociable women. (None of the subjects had any previous diagnosis of cancer at the beginning of the study.) No statistically significant increases in cancer risk were observed for the men in this study, but similar results were obtained in another long-term study that followed only male subjects. From 1948 to 1964, a battery of psychological tests was given to more than one thousand male medical students at Johns Hopkins University in Baltimore. The tests included a set of Rorschach inkblots, ambiguous images that reveal emotional attitudes through the pictures that subjects see in them. Descriptions of one blot, for example, ranged from "a young couple kissing" to "two people shaking hands," "two dancers," "two dogs snarling at each other," and "two cannibals boiling Macbeth in a kettle." In 1986 psychologist Pirkko Graves and her colleagues reported on an evaluation of the responses on the basis of well-adjusted or withdrawn and distant patterns of social interaction. (The answers to the sample inkblot listed above, for example, were rated $+5$, $+3$, 0, -3, and -5, respectively.) When the subjects' personality traits were compared to their health records, the students characterized as "loners," who suppressed their emotions, were sixteen times more likely to develop cancer than those who displayed their emotions and sometimes took active measures to relieve frustrations or anger. The most striking correlations between personality and cancer were observed for cancers of the blood cells, the digestive system, and the lymphatic system. Slight relationships were observed for cancers of the bladder, kidney, prostate, brain, and thyroid, and no correlation was observed for lung and skin cancers (the two types most likely to be caused by environmental factors), as well as such diseases as coronary heart disease, duodenal ulcers, and hypertension.

Some cancer physicians have tried to apply the findings of psychoneuroimmunological studies in practical terms. They urge their patients to use mental imagery in fighting their disease, picturing the cancer cells as weak and confused and visualizing the strong, vigorous white cells victoriously battling against them. The particular images used are a matter of personal preference: Some patients may view the white blood cells as soldiers battling the enemy; others see the white cells as hungry sharks gobbling up small, frightened

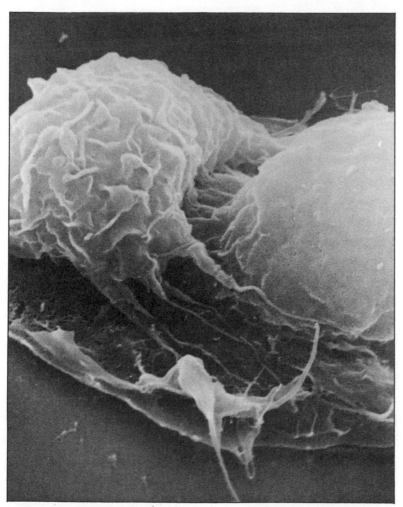

Microscopic battle: An activated mouse macrophage (on the left) is engulfing a mouse melanoma tumor cell, as shown in a scanning electron micrograph.

fish (the cancer cells). There is even a video game called "Killer T Cell," devised to aid the imagination. And medical workers are advised to be careful about saying negative things in front of patients, even patients under anesthcsia or in a coma, who may be able to hear and remember although they seem to have no awareness. Some surgeons are trying positive suggestions to help speed their patients' recovery from operations.

Recently some medical researchers, calling such ideas "folklore," have challenged the idea that negative attitudes can contribute to disease and positive ones can aid in recovery. They point out that not all studies support such findings, and the long-term studies that seem to show correlations between personality or social isolation and cancer may have other explanations. The socially isolated women of Alameda County, for example, may have had poor diets and suffered from vitamin deficiencies that left their bodies more vulnerable to cancer. Moreover, the critics say, the emphasis on personality factors in disease may have some bad effects. Some patients may be caused needless suffering and guilt, believing that falling ill was somehow their own fault. Others may be prompted to rely on "mental attitude" instead of getting the medical treatments they need. Psychoneuroimmunological approaches should be used as a supplement to conventional treatments, not as the only treatment.

Treatments and approaches designed to strengthen and stimulate the immune system are based on the assumption that the patient's immune defenses are still capable of responding. But some patients, especially those with advanced cancers, are in such poor condition that their immune systems cannot respond to stimulation. Some researchers have been trying to use the principle of *passive immunity* to treat such patients: to supply them with ready-made antibodies that might be able to bring the cancer under control long enough for the patients' own defenses to recover.

One approach in using passive immunity is to produce cancer vaccines from the blood of people who have won their own fights against cancer. Sometimes, for no reason that doctors can find, cancer patients who are very ill—even dying—suddenly get better. Their tumors shrink and disappear, and no traces of cancer cells can be found in their bodies. These mysterious cures, which unfortunately are very rare, are called *spontaneous remissions*. Doctors have been trying to find substances in the blood of such patients that will help to produce remissions in other cancer patients. They are also trying to find anticancer substances in the blood of healthy people who have built up an immunity to various forms of cancer.

One such substance is called *transfer factor*. It can be prepared from the lymphocytes of people who have an immunity to the antigens of a particular kind of cancer. (The relatives and close friends of cancer patients are especially likely to have antibodies against the patients' cancer. Some researchers consider this finding as further evidence that such cancers are caused by viruses.) Transfer factors appear to be a combination of an unusual type of RNA with a small proteinlike substance. Immunologists at the University of California in San Francisco and at the University of Michigan have studied the effects of transfer factor on patients with the bone cancer osteosarcoma. In these studies, one of them over a period of more than six years, patients who received injections of transfer factor after their tumors were removed by surgery or treated with radiation showed a somewhat higher survival rate and remained disease free for longer periods of time than those who received only the conventional treatments. Transfer factor produced positive effects on survival even though tests showed no change in the patients' own immunity against cancer after the treatments.

Passive immunity approaches have proved very useful in protecting people from bacterial and viral diseases. Immune gamma globulin, for example, may be given to people who have been exposed to disease-causing microbes, to keep them from becoming ill. So far such approaches have not proved very valuable in the treatment of cancer. A new variation, however, is one of the most active fields in medical research today. This is the use of *monoclonal antibodies*, which are revolutionizing not only the cancer field but many other areas of biology and medicine as well. It seems ironic that these powerful new weapons against cancer are actually produced from cancer cells.

Monoclonal antibodies were first devised in 1975 by British

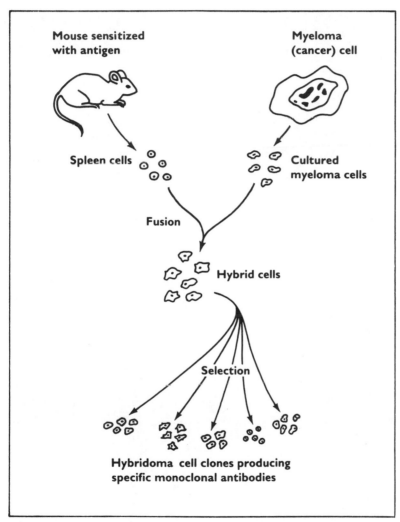

Hybridomas, produced by cell fusion, manufacture monoclonal antibodies specific for a single antigen.

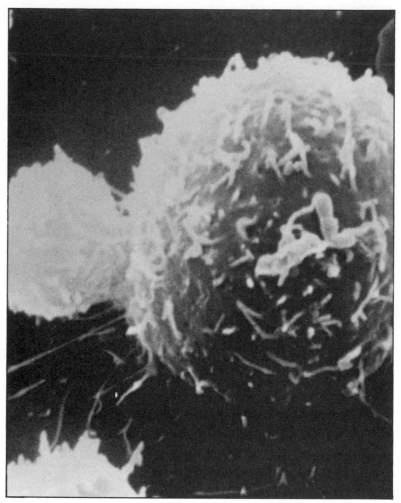

Scanning electron micrograph of cell fusion in progress. The small round cell is a spleen lymphocyte, and the large cell is a myeloma cell. The two cells will fuse into a single hybrid cell, or hybridoma.

researcher Cesar Milstein and his colleagues. The research team was working on mouse antibodies, produced by injecting foreign substances into mice. Milstein wanted to study the antibody-producing cells from mouse spleens. But when he tried to grow these cells in culture dishes, he found that they did not grow well and soon died out. Milstein came up with an ingenious idea that eventually won him a Nobel Prize. Cancer cells grow very well in culture, he reasoned; in fact, unlike normal cells, they go on growing and dividing indefinitely. Today's researchers are still using cells from some "immortal" cancer cell lines that have been maintained continuously, from generation to generation, for many decades. So why not combine a hardy, fast-growing cancer cell with one of the finicky spleen cells Milstein wanted to study? Perhaps the resulting hybrid cells would have the hardiness of their cancer "parent" while still retaining characteristics of their spleen cell "parent."

That is exactly what happened. Using special techniques for fusing cells, Milstein combined mouse spleen cells with cancer cells of a type called *myeloma*. The hardy, fast-growing hybrid cells that he obtained produced antibodies—the same kind of antibodies produced by the spleen cells. Milstein named these hybrid cells *hybridomas*.

The hybridomas turned out to be a mixture of cells producing various antibodies. Milstein separated them, and starting with individual cells, each producing only one particular kind of antibody, he produced *clones*: masses of cells all derived from a single parent cell and thus all sharing the same heredity. Each cell clone produced only one kind of antibody, and thus the antibodies they produced were named monoclonal ("one clone") antibodies. This was the first time such pure antibodies had ever been produced. (The antibodies produced by normal vaccines are complex mixtures.)

Monoclonal antibodies have applications in many fields of medicine. They are being used as sensitive tests for viruses, bacteria, and other microbes. A monoclonal antibody test has been developed for heart attacks, using antibodies against the protein *myosin*, which is released into the blood from a damaged heart muscle. In the cancer field, monoclonals are being used both in diagnostic tests and in bold new treatments. They are also proving invaluable in the biotechnology industry, since they make it possible to separate and purify body chemicals that are present in very tiny amounts in complicated mixtures. They are already being used to isolate and purify interferon and other biologicals used in cancer treatment.

Researchers in various laboratories have found a number of specific antigens on the surface of cancer cells and have produced monoclonal antibodies against them. Each kind of cancer has a number of different antigens, and different kinds of cancers have different sets of antigens. Some of the cancer antigens stay on the surface of the cancer cells, but others are shed into the blood. So two kinds of tests for cancer can be developed. Monoclonal antibodies against the antigens that cancer cells shed can be used for blood tests that show not only if a person has cancer, but what kind. The biotechnology firm Centocor, for example, has developed blood tests for pancreatic, liver, stomach, and ovarian cancers, based on the use of monoclonals. Antibodies against antigens that remain on the surface of cancer cells can be "tagged" with a small amount of radioactive substance and injected into the body. The antibodies are carried in the bloodstream until they reach the tumor, and then they latch onto the cancer cells. With a radiation detector, the doctor can find the location of the tagged tumors. Such tests are especially valuable in determining whether a tumor has metastasized. In one study of patients with colorectal cancers, monoclonal antibodies against a cancer antigen called *carcinoembryonic antigen* (CEA) were tagged with radioactive iodine. Injections of these antibodies detected 70 percent of the tumors. Even more encouraging, in four of the patients the monoclonal antibodies revealed tiny metastatic tumors, which could not be seen by any other imaging techniques. Tests on patients with melanoma, lymphoma, breast tumors, and prostate cancer, using monoclonal antibodies against different tumor antigens, gave equally good results.

Since monoclonal antibodies against cancer antigens zero in on the cancer cells in the body, they also provide ways to treat cancer. Monoclonal antibodies bind to cancer cells and stop them from multiplying, but by themselves they do not usually kill the cancer cells. By combining the monoclonals with radioisotopes or with poisons such as *ricin*, however, doctors can use these antibodies as ultraspecific delivery systems: The combinations attack only cancer cells and leave normal cells alone. Monoclonal antibodies bonded to radioactive iodine have shrunk liver tumors and other cancers and brought about stable remissions. Armed with ricin, an extract of the castor bean, monoclonals have acted as miniature guided missiles that knock out leukemia cells and stop the growth of tumors in patients with metastatic melanoma.

7. Frontiers of Cancer Research

When the United States officially declared war on cancer with the signing of the National Cancer Act in 1971, researchers were still groping in the dark. They did not have any clear idea of what cancer is and what causes normal cells to turn malignant. Many of the efforts to find treatments and cures took the form of testing things at random; researchers hoped that by chance they would hit on something that worked. Some specialists in the field were actually dubious about the whole idea of pouring more money into cancer research. They were afraid that most of the money would be wasted on poorly thought out desperation efforts and blind alleys, and that the best minds and talents would be lured away from basic research that could ultimately have applications not only in cancer but in many other areas of biology and medicine as well. We need to know more about how cells work, they counseled. If we find out more about the nature of cancer cells and their activities and how they differ from normal cells, then we will begin to get a handle on the cancer problem. Instead of striking out blindly, we will be able to use what we have learned to find cancer's weak points and to devise ways to strike at them.

Fortunately, the worst fears of the cancer researchers did not come true. There was some waste in the government-sponsored programs, but a lot of good basic research was done. Out of this research grew the oncogene theory that is helping to put the whole cancer picture in perspective. Meanwhile, the explosive development of recombinant DNA, monoclonal antibodies, and other areas of biotechnology provided researchers with new tools for study and new therapies that had not even been dreamed of back in 1971.

One focus of current cancer research is at the genetic level. Cancer-causing oncogenes are being identified, isolated, mapped on the chromosomes, and studied. Researchers hope that an understanding of how such genes act will give them clues to ways of intervening. Perhaps they will be able to turn off certain key genes, or counteract their products, so that the development of normal cells into cancer cells can be short-circuited.

Studies of oncogenes can have some other important applications, too. In a study of children with neuroblastoma, sponsored by the National Cancer Institute, researchers at several medical schools found that some of the children had only one copy of a particular oncogene (called *N-myc*) in their cells, while others had more than one. Seventy percent of the children with only a single copy of this oncogene survived for at least eighteen months, without any progressive growth of their cancers. But those whose cancer cells had from three to ten copies of the gene had only a 30-percent chance of surviving that long after diagnosis without growth of their cancers, and those whose cells had more than ten copies of the *N-myc* gene had only a 5-percent chance. The most striking differences were found in children with very advanced, Stage IV cancers at the time their disease was first diagnosed. In Stage IV there are typically large, solid tumors that have spread to numerous sites in the body. Yet in most children with only a single copy of the oncogene, even these advanced cancers continued to grow very slowly. The presence of multiple copies of this oncogene thus provides a good prediction of the future course of the disease and alerts doctors to cases in which the cancer can be expected to grow very quickly, so that it should be treated very aggressively. With only a single copy of the gene present, there is more time for gentler treatments.

Researchers in Japan have reported the discovery and isolation of an oncogene responsible for metastasis. They used monoclonal antibodies to find and bind to antigens on the surface of cancer cells, then tested the antibodies to see if any could stop the spread of cancers in mice. One antibody was very effective indeed, and the researchers worked backward from the cancer antigen it had located to the gene controlling its formation. They hope that by studying the gene, they will learn more about metastasis and how to stop it.

About thirty human oncogenes have already been found, but in 1986 researchers at Massachusetts Institute of Technology and their associates announced a first: the discovery of a gene that *prevents* the development of cancer. They were studying *retinoblastoma*, a cancer of the eye, which usually strikes children in their first few years. The researchers were looking for differences in the chromosomes, the structures in the cell nucleus that contain the genes. Cells normally have twenty-three pairs of chromosomes, two of each kind. Each kind has a characteristic size and shape and markings; when the nucleus of a cell is photographed under high magnification, scientists can actually sort out the chromosomes in the picture for convenient study and comparison. Carefully examining the chromosomes of children with retinoblastoma, researchers discovered that a portion of chromosome 13 was often missing in the cells of such children. A gene that is normally found in that part of the chromosome works to inhibit cell growth. Since there are two chromosome 13's in each cell, even if the gene is missing on one of them, the gene on the other produces enough of its growth-inhibiting product to keep the cells normal. An accident might happen, early in a child's development—perhaps damage by a chemical or by radiation—to knock out the growth-inhibiting gene in one of the eye cells. When the growth-inhibiting genes are missing on both chromosomes of the thirteenth pair, cells in the eyes begin to run wild, growing out of control and forming a cancerous tumor.

The discovery of a cancer-inhibiting gene leads to a lot of new information about normal and cancer cells. It may also lead to some practical applications: first of all, a test for identifying people with hereditary forms of retinoblastoma and perhaps a chromosome-screening test for people whose children might be at risk of developing the disease; and secondly, possible treatments. With the identification of the gene, researchers will be able to find the protein this gene produces and study its action. They may be able to supply the missing protein and turn the cancer cells back into normal cells; or, using techniques of gene therapy that are being developed, they may be able to replace the missing gene.

Researchers at the University of Cincinnati and elsewhere are on the trail of another cancer-inhibiting gene. They have found that children with the hereditary growth disorder *Beckwith-Wiedemann syndrome* have a higher risk of developing three types of cancer, affecting the kidney, the liver, and muscle cells. All patients with such tumors were found to be carrying a particular *mutant* (changed) gene on chromosome 11. In tumor cells, the same mutant gene was observed on both members of the chromosome 11 pair, while in normal cells from the same patients only one chromosome of the pair carried the mutation. The researchers suggest that just as for retinoblastoma, inheriting one copy of the mutant gene makes a person more susceptible to the cancers, but a change must also occur in the other chromosome of the pair for a tumor actually to develop. This gene is needed for cells to differentiate properly. (Cells in which the gene is missing entirely, rather than just changed, remain in an undeveloped, embryolike state, while cells with two copies of the normal gene develop into liver or kidney or muscle cells in the usual way.)

Studies being conducted at the University of California at Irvine and at the University of Southern California in Los Angeles suggest that there is indeed something important about chromosome 11. The scientists have been investigating lines of hybrid cells in culture. When two cells are fused to form a hybrid, and then the double cell is cloned, producing generations of cell offspring, the successive daughter cells tend to lose some of their chromosomes. When the researchers produced hybrids between normal cells and cancer cells from kidney tumors like the ones found in the Cincinnati patients, the daughter cells promptly differentiated, losing their tumor-forming ability. They looked just like normal cells. But in later generations, some of the daughter cells became cancerous again. Microscopic examination revealed that they had lost chromosome 11. Since they no longer had a normal gene to counteract the cancer-causing mutant gene, they turned back into cancer cells.

The search for *differentiators*—drugs and biological agents that cause cancer cells to turn back into normal cells—is a very active area of cancer research today. More than 250 substances that can cause cancer cells to differentiate in a test tube or culture dish have already been discovered. They range from vitamin A and the related retinoids to *benzo-diazepines*, a group of tranquilizers that includes diazepam (commonly known by its trade name, Valium). Even some of the *cytotoxic* drugs, now being used to kill cancer cells, can turn them back into normal cells when used in small doses. One synthetic chemical, *hexamethylene bisacetamide* (HMBA), produces differentiation in many different types of cancer cells, including those of leukemias, melanomas, and colon and bladder cancers. They seem to turn off several genes that promote uncontrolled cell growth, while turning on genes that produce normal cell proteins.

One of the natural substances that helps to normalize cancer cells in tissue culture experiments is a protein called *concanavalin A* (Con A), found in bean meal. Max Burger at Princeton University has found that Con A sticks to the surface of certain kinds of cancer cells, like a "chemical Band-Aid." When the surface of a cancer cell growing in a dish is covered with this protein, the cell stops growing wildly and behaves more like a normal cell. If the Con A coating is taken off, the cell becomes cancerous again.

Even the best of the differentiators found so far do not work on all the cancer cells. When HMBA is tested on animals with cancer, for example, about 95 percent of the malignant cells become normalized, but there is no effect on about 5 percent. Researchers have noted that some differentiators, like HMBA, work on the cell nucleus, while others, such as Con A, may work on the cell membrane. They hope that by teaming up two or more differentiators that work in different ways, they will be able to return 100 percent of the cancer cells to normalcy. Differentiators may also make conventional chemotherapy more effective. By combining conventional drugs with differentiators, oncologists may be able to use smaller doses of the drugs and thus cut down the harmful side effects.

Researchers comparing notes at a National Institutes of Health workshop late in 1985 discovered that their studies all pointed to the same explanation of how tumor cells resist drug treatments. The resistant cells pump out the drugs as fast as they enter, so the anticancer drugs do not have time to damage the malignant cells. A special membrane protein called *P-glycoprotein* often appears to work in this pumping mechanism. Resistant cancer cells may have many copies of the gene for the P-glycoprotein. The more copies of the gene, the more protein is made and built into the cell membrane, and the more effectively the cells can resist the action of drugs. This discovery points to a way to make cancer chemotherapy more effective: If researchers can make an antibody or drug that binds to the P-glycoprotein and puts it out of action, then the cell membrane will no longer be able to pump out the drugs.

Loyola University researcher Leonard Erickson believes that some cancer cells become drug resistant by producing large amounts of a "repair enzyme" that repairs the damage produced by drugs. After performing successful in vitro tests, Erickson and his colleagues are now testing a naturally occurring fungus product called *streptozotocin* on a group of patients with gastrointestinal cancer. Streptozotocin ties up the cancer repair enzymes; in laboratory tests it increased the number of cells killed by chemotherapy by a factor of 1,000 to 10,000 compared to chemotherapy alone.

A husband-and-wife team working at the University of Washington in Seattle, Karl and Ingegerd Hellstrom, have been studying one of the ways that cancer cells elude the body's defenses. The cells produce substances called *blocking factors*, perhaps antigens shed from the cell surface, that attach themselves to lymphocytes and stop them from attacking and killing the cancer cells. The Hellstroms have found that the blood of about 85 percent of blacks and that of some white patients in remission from melanoma contain an *unblocking factor*—an antibody against the blocking factor that frees the lymphocytes and permits them to attack and kill melanoma cells. Blood plasma from black donors is being used experimentally to treat melanoma patients.

Another of the cancer cells' defenses against the immune system was discovered by researchers at the University of Minnesota. They found that cancer cells have more of a substance called *sialic acid* on their surface than normal cells do. The researchers suggested that large amounts of this sialic acid somehow prevented the body's immune system from fighting such cancer cells. It was also found that an enzyme called *vibrio cholera neuraminidase* (VCN), taken from the bacterium that causes cholera, can remove sialic acid from the surface of cells. The Minnesota research team theorized that stripping the excess sialic acid from the surface of cancer cells by treating them with VCN, then injecting them back into the patient, would permit the patient's immune system to make antibodies against the cancer cells. Some promising results have been obtained in experiments with mice. In human cancer patients, injections of VCN-treated tumor cells have caused small tumors to shrink and helped to produce remissions in leukemia patients. The VCN treatments are more effective when used after surgery or radiation therapy, or in combination with chemotherapy. Work on VCN is still preliminary, however, and it is currently more of a research tool than a practical cancer treatment.

Studies of cancer cell biology are bringing new insights into metastasis. In order to reach the bloodstream and migrate to new locations, cancer cells must first burrow through the normal tissues and penetrate through the *basement membrane*, a tough elastic barrier between tissues. Researchers have found that the cells secrete enzymes that cut a path through the tissues, and then they bind to a cross-shaped protein called *laminin*, which stimulates them to release other enzymes that dissolve the basement membrane. These cancer enzymes, isolated with the aid of monoclonal antibodies, are now being studied.

Meanwhile, National Cancer Institute researchers reported in 1986 that they had discovered a protein produced by tumor cells that enables the cells to move around. They isolated this protein, which they named *autocrine motility factor* (AMF), from human melanoma cells that had migrated from the skin to brain tissue. When AMF was added to melanoma cells growing in laboratory dishes, the cells began to move, even squeezing through small pores in a filter. Lance Liotta, the leader of the research group, suggests that AMF may become the basis for a blood test to detect the presence or spread of cancer. Its blood levels might indicate how metastatic the cancer is. And if scientists are able to produce inhibitors that stop the action of AMF, they might be able to prevent localized cancers from metastasizing.

In the early 1970's, Harvard researcher Judah Folkman discovered a substance in tumor cells that stimulates the rapid growth of new blood capillaries. The tumors utilize this substance, which Folkman named *tumor angiogenesis factor* (TAF), to provide themselves with a rich blood supply. The Monsanto Company provided financing for a major research effort by the Harvard team to isolate and study TAF and perhaps to find a way to block it and starve out the cancer cells. The study was long and frustrating. For a while, researchers began to doubt that TAF really existed. Ultimately, TAF turned out to be a group of proteins, and a research team at the Salk Institute in San Diego finally announced the structure of one of them in 1985. Meanwhile, the Harvard researchers, headed by Bert Vallee, discovered an entirely different protein that triggers the growth of new blood vessels around cancer cells. The protein, named *angiogenin*, was isolated from a human colon cancer. Its complete structure was worked out, and then the researchers isolated the gene that produces it and cloned the gene by recombinant DNA techniques.

Angiogenin has some exciting possibilities. It may be the basis for a new cancer test. Blockers for angiogenin might prevent the growth of solid tumors; they might also be useful in protecting diabetics from blindness, which sometimes develops as a result of abnormal blood-vessel growth. Angiogenin itself may be used to promote the growth of new blood vessels after a heart attack and to speed recovery from burns and other severe tissue damage.

Although many cancer researchers are conducting their studies at the level of the microscopic cancer cell, or the genes and chemicals inside it, others are focusing on the effects of cancer on the body as a whole.

New Jersey oncologist Dennis Devereux is speculating on why cancer kills its victims. Uncontrolled growth of cancer cells cannot be the whole story, he points out, asking, "Why should one percent of the body weight of the host kill the host?" Devereux is studying the ways that cancer cells interfere with the body's metabolism. He has isolated a product of cancer cells that interferes with the healing of wounds by preventing normal cells called *fibroblasts* from producing *collagen*, the protein that provides the framework for the new healing growth. Cancer patients' wounds do not heal as well as normal people's, and thus it is difficult for them to recover from surgery. Another cell product in cancer patients causes both humans and animals to lose fats and proteins, producing the "wasting away" that is typical of cancer patients.

The medical term for this wasting away is cachexia, and it can be extremely severe. Patients with advanced cancer may lose an average of 16 percent of their body weight. The cancer cells compete for nutrients with the normal body cells, and their appetite is enormous. The cancer cell's mechanisms for generating energy are very inefficient. Cancer patients convert the proteins in their body tissues to *glucose*, the sugar the cancer cells need for energy, and enormous amounts of energy and calories are used up in the process.

Joseph Gold, director of the Syracuse Cancer Research Institute, suggested in 1969 that *hydrazine sulfate*, a common industrial chemical used to fuel rockets, clean boilers, and kill insects, could help to solve the problem of cachexia by improving cancer patients' glucose metabolism. Practitioners of "unorthodox medicine" quickly picked up the suggestion, and their support gave hydrazine sulfate the reputation of a "fringe" medicine. For many years, most members of the medical community were suspicious of the treatment. But in the 1980's hydrazine sulfate gained some respectability when reputable scientists reported studies with encouraging results. This chemical is not a cancer cure; it does not attack cancer cells or cause tumors to shrink. According to some studies, it may help to normalize cancer patients' use of food substances and energy. In one study at the University of California, Los Angeles (UCLA), nearly half of a group of patients with advanced cancers showed an increase in glucose levels, and their weight loss stopped; some even gained back some of the weight they had lost. Many members of the medical community, however, still doubt that hydrazine sulfate has any therapeutic value.

Cancer researchers in Cooperstown, New York, have recently made the surprising discovery that tumors in rats grew two to four times faster when the rats were not fed for twenty-four hours. Considering the high demands of cancer cells for food and energy, the researchers had expected the opposite result—that the growth rate would be faster when the food supply was increased, apparently satisfying their needs. Yet when the fasting rats were fed, the growth rate of the tumors slowed down again. The researchers speculate that the tumor cells may produce some substance that decreases cancer patients' appetite, causing them to cut back on their food intake and thus stimulating faster tumor growth.

Another perplexing finding about tumor growth may have several explanations. Some researchers have observed that patients with lung, breast, and colorectal cancer who receive blood transfusions are more likely to have recurrences of cancer after surgery and are less likely to survive than those who were not given blood. The researchers suggest that the blood transfusions, containing numerous foreign antigens, weakened the patients' immune systems. Another possibility is suggested by studies indicating that tumor growth is stimulated by iron supplements. Researchers at the University of Florida–Gainesville say that anemia in cancer patients may actually be a body defense, and that their bodies remove iron from the blood and store it away in the liver in an attempt to starve out the cancer cells. Perhaps it is the extra iron in blood transfusions that promotes the recurrence of tumors, rather than (or in addition to) the effects on the immune system.

In laboratories in various parts of the world, researchers are trying a number of innovative approaches to cancer treatment. At Memorial Sloan-Kettering Cancer Center in New York, urologists testing high-energy *shock waves* to destroy kidney stones discovered that these shock waves also killed or stopped the growth of cancer cells in test tubes and in animals. At Boston University Hospital, researchers have used recombinant DNA techniques to combine the poisonous *diphtheria toxin* with a hormone to produce a weapon against melanoma. The hormone zeroes in on the melanoma cells, and the toxin attacks them, leaving healthy skin cells unharmed. Researchers in Tulsa, Oklahoma, and in Brussels, Belgium, treated cancer patients and AIDS patients with a natural body substance called *met-enkephalin*. This substance, which has an opiumlike pain-killing effect, improves the activity of T cells and natural killer cells, making the immune defenses more effective. The met-enkephalin treatments had no harmful side effects. Researchers believe that combining the substance with other immune stimulators may produce even better results.

A series of studies by researchers at Pennsylvania State University suggests that the *opioids*, the group of natural pain killers to which met-enkephalin belongs, may play a fundamental role in regulating tumor cells. The Penn State group has found that a variety of human tumors contain both opioids and cell membrane receptors for them. Opioid receptors are also found on newly developing nerve tissue, and opioids play a role in slowing brain development in rat embryos. These studies grew out of earlier work in which the researchers found that only one third of a group of mice injected with nerve cancer cells developed tumors when they were also given injections of opioids. (In a group that did not receive opioids, all the mice injected with cancer cells developed tumors.) The recent studies show that this natural growth regulation is not restricted to nerve cells and their tumors; it may be applied to other forms of cancer as well.

At the University of California, San Diego (UCSD), researchers have developed a method of growing tumor specimens from cancer patients in a jellylike medium. In this gel, the cultured tumors grow very much the same way they do in the body, forming a three-dimensional tissue structure, genetic makeup, and cell growth patterns typical of cancer. Testing drugs on such tumor cultures should provide results more similar to the effects in the body than are given by the conventional tests on tumor cells growing in a culture dish or flask. The UCSD researchers have been successful in growing twenty types of human cancers, including lung, colon, and ovarian tumors.

In 1985, a research and development firm called Biotherapeutics, Inc., opened for business. The firm, founded by two former National Cancer Institute researchers, uses front-line techniques to tailor-make treatments for individual cancer patients. For charges ranging from $1,500 to $35,000, Biotherapeutics oncologists will analyze a patient's tumor cells and develop treatments that may include the use of monoclonal antibodies, immunoconjugates, and lymphokines. For one patient, white blood cells may be activated with lymphokines like interleukin-2, then tested to see if they attack the patient's tumor cells. For another, an individual tumor cell vaccine may be prepared. Experts in medical ethics have expressed doubts about whether such private research-for-pay companies should exist. But, the firm's founders point out, "Patients aren't interested in what research will do for society in ten years; they want to know what research will do for them tomorrow." There is also a basic difference in philosophy: Government and university scientists work with the idea that all cancers of a particular type are similar, and a general treatment can be developed for each form. Biotherapeutics is based on the premise that each patient's cancer is unique and requires an individualized approach.

The successes that cancer researchers have achieved so far are generating a number of social and bioethical problems that did not exist a decade or two ago. Now that a number of cancers have become treatable and even curable, there are millions of cancer survivors alive. Yet the old attitudes of fear and secrecy have not entirely disappeared. Recovered cancer patients often find themselves victims of discrimination. When they try to return to their old jobs, they may meet with excuses and efforts to get them to take early retirement; coworkers and friends may act uncomfortable, as though they thought cancer was "catching." The enormous expense for cancer treatments may have exhausted the cancer patient's insurance coverage and drained away the whole family's life savings. The cancer, or the treatments, may have caused disability or disfigurement, to which the cancer survivor and others must adjust. And because cancer can recur, even many years after it has seemed to disappear, the recovered cancer patient must live under a shadow of potential death.

There are some forms of help available. For cancer patients facing the effects of prejudice and fear, the American Cancer Society offers a booklet, "Cancer: Your Job, Insurance and the Law. 84-100M-4585-PS," which provides an overview of the patient's legal rights. Recently a bimonthly news magazine called *Cope* has been launched as a "consumer publication for cancer patients, their families and physicians." The magazine provides news and features on all aspects of living cancer and the latest developments in cancer prevention and treatment. The subscription rate is $20 per year or $35 for two years. For subscription or other information, call 1-800-343-COPE (303-238-5035 in Colorado) or write to:

> Cope
> 12600 West Colfax Avenue, Suite B-400
> Denver, CO 80215

8. Our Dangerous World

Hopeful news on the cancer front has been coming out of research laboratories and hospitals. New treatments and new combinations of treatments are saving the lives of thousands of people who would have been doomed only a year or two ago. Yet year after year, the cancer death rate has been steadily going up. The number of cancer deaths gets higher every year, and more peeple are getting cancer than ever before.

Why are so many people still dying of cancer when so many are being saved? Some experts say that it is because fewer people are dying of other diseases—more are living long enough to get cancer. But that is only part of the answer. Many researchers believe that the continuing rise in the cancer death rate is our own fault. By polluting our world and abusing our bodies, we are literally killing ourselves.

Smoke and gases pour out of cars, factories, and homes. The lungs of the modern city dweller are blackened by soot deposits, but air pollution is not a problem confined to cities. Toxic chemicals and soot particles are carried through the atmosphere all over the world—even out over the oceans and to the most deserted parts of the ice-covered polar regions. Tons of chemical wastes spill out of factory drainpipes, and pesticides are washed off the farmlands by the rain into rivers and lakes. These waste materials are taken in by tiny water creatures, which in turn are eaten by fish, moving up the food chain in increasing concentrations until they get into the human diet. Various industries accumulate toxic wastes and try to bury them safely underground where they cannot harm anyone; but sometimes there are leaks. When a housing development was built on a landfill in the Love Canal section of Niagara Falls, New York, the seal over a toxic waste deposit was disturbed and a variety of poisonous chemicals began to seep out into the soil and water. Eventually, the government had to declare the whole area uninhabitable, and the people who lived there had to move away. Scattered around the country are many more buried toxic waste depots—no one even knows how many, or where they all are, or when another major leak will occur.

With all the pollution in our world, it is not surprising that scientists have found carcinogens in the food we eat, the water we drink, and the air we breathe. For instance, every car that goes by gives off a bit of benzpyrene into the air. This is the same carcinogen that cancer researchers use to produce cancer in experimental mice. Residues of DDT and other pesticides in foods have also been shown to produce cancer in animals. It is hard to say how much of a risk these carcinogens pose for humans, because cancer takes a long time to develop in people—often several decades; but a National Academy of Sciences report has recently estimated that pesticide residues in foods may be responsible for as many as 20,000 cases of cancer in the United States each year.

Since the first atomic bombs were exploded at the end of World War II, we have become conscious of another danger in our world—radiation pollution. Our earth has always had a certain amount of natural radiation from rocks and soil; in fact, in certain parts of the country where the ground contains deposits of uranium ores and other radioactive minerals, there is a growing concern about *radon*, a radioactive gas that can pollute the air of homes and workplaces. Rays from the sun and from outer space also contribute to the natural radiation background. But atomic explosions produce large amounts of radioisotopes that get into the water and soil and are taken up by plants and then by animals that eat the plants. These radiations can cause cancer by changing the DNA and other substances in our cells. Most of the nations of the world have now agreed not to test nuclear weapons in the atmosphere, where they would add to the radiation pollution. But some radiations last a long time, and they are still around from the explosions and tests that took place before the test bans took effect in 1963. Now that atomic energy is being used for power plants and various other peaceful purposes, there is a danger that radiation pollution may increase. Nuclear energy has had an impressive safety record in general, but there is always the danger that a combination of accidents and human errors may lead to a meltdown. The first major nuclear reactor accident occurred at Chernobyl, in the Soviet Union, in 1986 and sent a radioactive cloud drifting over much of that country and neighboring countries. Cases of leukemia and other forms of cancer due to the Chernobyl accident will be turning up for many years to come. And even without accidents, nuclear reactors produce radioactive wastes, adding to the problems and dangers of toxic waste disposal.

The atomic radiations are not the only source of radiation-caused cancers. The use of X rays for medical purposes has become very common, and though the amount of radiation a person receives in a single diagnostic X ray is very small and not dangerous in itself, scientists believe that radiation exposures gradually add up. People who like to sunbathe or who go to tanning salons may get heavy doses of ultraviolet radiation. Recently the experts have noticed that the ozone layer in the upper atmosphere, which helps to filter out the ultraviolet rays of sunlight before they can reach the earth's surface, has been getting thinner. Part of the drop appears to be due to natural fluctuations in the sun's activity, but a substantial fraction may be due to pollution. The chlorofluorocarbons that were used in aerosol sprays may have contributed to the erosion of our protective ozone cover. The U.S. Environmental Protection Agency has recently estimated that if the destruction of the ozone layer continues, the number of cases of skin cancer will double in the next eighty-eight years.

Many people are exposed to cancer-causing chemicals in their work. Asbestos workers have been found to have a high risk of developing a certain kind of abdominal and chest cancer called *mesothelioma*, as well as colon and lung cancer. Even members of asbestos workers' families have a higher-than-average risk of developing mesotheliomas. People who live in communities where there are copper-smelting factories have a higher-than-average risk of lung cancer. A chemical called *vinyl chloride*, used to produce polyvinyl chloride plastics, has been shown to cause cancer in some plastics factory workers. In three Ohio towns where industries using vinyl chloride were located, researchers found an unusual number of deaths from cancers of the brain and nerves.

The foods we eat and the beverages we drink bring more possible dangers. More than three thousand different chemicals are added to the foods we eat—as coloring or flavoring agents, to change the texture of foods, to make whipped toppings foam, to keep foods from spoiling or caking or turning liquid. Laws give the federal Food and Drug Administration (FDA) the power to oversee the testing of food additives and to prevent the use of any found to be harmful. In particular, a law called the *Delaney Amendment*, passed in 1958, states that no agent that causes cancer in any animal can be added to foods. This law was used by the FDA to make food manufacturers stop using a dye called Red No. 2, found in jellies, soft drinks, dog food, and even in cottage cheese (for some strange reason, this red dye makes dairy products whiter), after animal experiments showed it can cause cancer. Another widely used food additive that was banned after it was found to cause cancer in animals was the artificial sweetener cyclamate. But when the FDA tried to ban the sweetener saccharin on similar grounds, public protests made the government agency back down.

The question of carcinogens in foods is not as clear-cut as the Delaney Amendment might make it seem. A chemical that causes cancer in certain kinds of animals might not be a carcinogen for other species, and thus there is some question of how valid a basis animal studies provide for drawing conclusions about effects on humans. In addition, there is the matter of concentration. In order to produce observable effects in a reasonable time, researchers typically feed animals very large doses of the chemical being tested—far larger than the normal diet would contain. For example, a person would have to drink a hundred bottles of diet beverage a day in order to consume an amount of sweetener comparable to the concentrations used in the animal tests. It is often observed that a substance in low concentrations might have effects on the body that are very different from those observed for the same substance at high concentrations—possibly even opposite effects.

Because of such reasonable doubts, as well as many years of use without any obvious ill effects, a number of possibly carcinogenic chemicals are still being added to our foods. *Sulfur dioxide*, used in food manufacturing (for example, to bleach raisins), is one of them. Another is *nitrite*, used in preserving cold cuts like corned beef and bologna. In the body, nitrite may be changed to chemicals called *nitrosamines*, which can act as carcinogens. Vitamin C has been found to block the formation of nitrosamines, and thus may provide some protection against the carcinogenic action of nitrite. The food additives *BHA* and *BHT*, used as antioxidants to prevent spoiling, may also provide some protection by inactivating potential carcinogens before they can harm the body.

Some carcinogens occur naturally in foods. Substances in smoked meats and fish are believed to cause stomach cancer. Hamburger and other meats that are broiled or fried well-done contain half a dozen chemicals (including benzpyrene) that may cause mutations or cancer. *Aflatoxin*, a mold product that may be found on peanuts and other nuts that have not been dried properly after harvesting, can cause liver cancer.

Some researchers believe that our whole modern diet may be one of the causes of certain kinds of cancer. In particular, the high fat content of the foods eaten in the United States and other affluent countries is suspect. People in Scotland, who eat a great deal of beef, have one of the highest rates of colon cancer in the world. In Japan, where people usually eat fish rather than beef, colon cancer is very rare. But when Japanese people move to the United States and begin to eat the American diet, their rate of colon cancer quickly rises to the high American level. Studies have also found a link between a high-fat diet and breast cancer.

Denis Burkitt, who first described and studied the virus-caused cancer Burkitt's lymphoma, came to some pioneering conclusions about diet and cancer on the basis of his observations in Africa. He suggested that by eating more fibrous foods, such as bran, whole-grain cereals, and fresh fruits and vegetables, people can help guard against colon and other cancers. When people eat a high-fiber diet, the remains of digested foods move through their intestines more rapidly, and there is less time for possible carcinogens to stay in contact with the large intestines. Fiber may also bind carcinogens, helping to carry them out of the body, and it may alter the population levels of the microorganisms that live in the intestines (the *microflora*), shifting the balance from forms that produce toxic chemicals to kinds that do not give off harmful products. Studies in a number of developing industrialized countries have generally supported the findings that colon cancer rates are low when there is a high fiber content in the diet and high among people whose diet contains large amounts of fats and little fiber.

Studies have shown that calcium in the diet can provide some protection against colon and rectal cancer. People who drink a lot of milk or eat dairy products have been found to have less colon cancer. In a recent study, researchers gave calcium tablets to people who had close family members with colon cancer. Before they started taking the calcium supplements, these people had a very high rate of new cell formation in the lining of their intestines, a condition linked with a high risk of colon cancer. But after they had been taking the calcium tablets for two or three months, the activity of their intestinal cells fell to a normal, healthy level.

Vegetables of the cabbage family, including broccoli, brussels sprouts, and cauliflower, as well as dried beans, have been found to decrease the risk of cancer. These vegetables contain chemicals that help to protect normal cells from carcinogens. In fact, researchers at Johns Hopkins University in Baltimore are testing some of these chemicals, called *dithiolthiones*, as protectors of healthy cells during radiation therapy and chemotherapy. The dithiolthiones were found to increase the levels of *glutathione* in the body tissues. This substance plays a key role in the conversion of food materials to energy in cells and also is involved in detoxifying harmful chemicals in the body.

Some drugs can cause cancer. In 1971, it was discovered that the daughters of women who took a synthetic sex hormone called *diethylstilbestrol* (DES) while they were pregnant were in danger of developing a deadly form of vaginal cancer. There have been reports that middle-aged women who took estrogen to ease the symptoms of menopause had a greatly increased risk of uterine cancer. Some studies seemed to indicate a link between the hormones in birth control pills and breast cancer, but the latest evidence is that the forms of birth control pills now being used do not increase the risk of breast cancer.

Alcoholic beverages can contribute to the development of cancer, especially cancers of the mouth, throat, esophagus, larynx, breast, and liver. The risk is even greater for heavy drinkers who are also smokers. Studies indicate that both alcohol and tobacco reduce the effectiveness of the immune system. (So does *tetrahydrocannabinol*, the active ingredient in marijuana.) This immune suppression probably contributes to the cancer-causing effects of drinking and smoking, along with their more direct damaging effects on the body tissues.

Every time someone smokes near you, the air you breathe is being polluted with benzpyrene and other dangerous carcinogens. But although your risk of getting cancer is increased by this "passive smoking," the smoker is being hurt far worse. In 1962, the Surgeon General of the U.S. Public Health Service set up a committee of scientists and doctors to study the relationship between smoking and health. After a long and careful study of all the scientific reports on smoking, the committee made its report in January 1964. It stated that cigarette smoking is a cause of lung cancer, and that pipe smoking can cause lip cancer. There also seems to be a relationship between smoking and cancers in other parts of the body. In addition to cancer, smoking can cause other diseases of the lungs and breathing passages and can be dangerous to people with heart trouble. (Recent studies suggest that in addition to the carcinogenic effects of the tars in cigarette smoke, nicotine itself can act as a cofactor promoting the metastasis of tumors.)

Since the Surgeon General's report, many other studies have found more evidence that smokers have a much higher chance of dying from lung cancer than people who do not smoke. In addition to statistical studies, which have all shown an increase in lung cancer rates following the increase in smoking rates, experiments have been conducted on animals trained to smoke cigarettes. At the Veterans Administration Hospital in East Orange, New Jersey, cancer researchers trained a group of beagles to smoke. At first, the smoke had to be pumped into the dogs' lungs. But then they grew to like smoking and even wagged their tails and begged for cigarettes. Some of the dogs became heavy smokers, smoking more than six thousand cigarettes in the test period of two and one-half years. At the end of the test period, the scientists examined the dogs. Many of the dogs that smoked developed lung cancer or died of other lung diseases. In a group of dogs of the same ages that did not smoke, none died and none had lung cancer.

Before these studies were conducted, many smokers who did not want to quit could say, "Those cancer reports are only statistics. Nobody has ever shown that smoking really causes cancer." That was true for a while, for in humans lung cancer takes so long to develop and people are exposed to so many other kinds of influences that statistical studies and even individual case histories could not completely prove that it was smoking that had caused a particular cancer. But now it seems sure, and smokers who do not believe the warning printed on each cigarette package are only fooling themselves.

Health warnings about the dangers of passive smoking, which can increase the cancer risk for close relatives of smokers and people who must work in the same room with smokers, have made nonsmokers increasingly militant. They have pushed through bans of smoking in public places in many localities. Such restrictions, as well as worries about the health hazard, have prompted many smokers to cut down on their smoking or to quit. Cigarette manufacturers have responded to the mood of their customers by producing brands with lower amounts of nicotine and cancer-causing tars, as well as brands with filter tips to remove harmful substances from the smoke. But these efforts may actually backfire: Nicotine is an addictive drug, and the smoker becomes accustomed to taking in a certain level of it each day. Smokers who switch to cigarettes with less nicotine have been found to inhale more deeply, take more puffs in the same length of time, and smoke their cigarettes down closer to the end, in an unconscious effort to get more nicotine. As a result, the smoker actually takes in *more* of the carcinogens from each cigarette.

Some worried smokers switch to "smokeless tobaccos," such as chewing tobacco and snuff. Baseball players who can be seen chewing and spitting on televised ball games have helped to popularize the image of chewing tobacco, and it is now being used even by some schoolchildren. But smokeless tobaccos have their own hazards. Chewing tobacco and snuff can cause cancers of the mouth and gastrointestinal tract, as well as heart disease and dental disease. The Surgeon General has declared that smokeless tobaccos present a health hazard rivaling that of smoking, and federal regulations now require warning labels on chewing tobacco and snuff, similar to those on cigarettes.

9. What You Can Do About Cancer

According to the cancer experts, between 60 and 90 percent of cancers have causes that can be found in our environment. The National Cancer Institute has estimated that about 40 percent of all cancer deaths are due to smoking. Diet accounts for 25 to 30 percent. Job-related factors cause another 10 percent, and 10 to 15 percent of all cancers are due to pollution.

So it is clear that to a great extent we have control over whether or not we and our loved ones will get cancer.

A sudden, dramatic drop in the cancer rate would come

about if *all* people would stop smoking. The Surgeon General believes that more than 350,000 people die prematurely each year because of smoking. About half of these are cancer deaths.

What should you do? It is obvious. Don't smoke. And try to persuade people you know to stop smoking, too.

Eating a sensible diet, high in fibers and low in fats, can also decrease your chances of getting cancer. Eat plenty of fresh fruits, vegetables (especially members of the cabbage family), whole-grain breads, and cereals, and drink milk or take in some other good calcium source.

Concerning carcinogens in the environment, you can find out what your community is doing to reduce pollution. Both federal and local governments are taking steps to clean up our environment. Government and industry spend billions of dollars a year in the fight against pollution. Through these efforts, our air is getting cleaner, and our water is getting purer. Stiffer government regulations are also helping to protect the health of workers.

For people who are unfortunate enough to get cancer, each year is bringing promising new treatments. But all the skill of cancer specialists and all the exciting new research discoveries cannot help if ignorance or fear keeps you away from your doctor until it is too late. Get acquainted with your own body and know the seven warning signals of cancer drawn up by the American Cancer Society:

Change in bowel or bladder habits.
A sore that does not heal.
Unusual bleeding or discharge.
Thickening or lump in the breast or elsewhere.
Indigestion or difficulty in swallowing.
Obvious change in a wart or mole.
Nagging cough or hoarseness.

For some helpful pamphlets and other information about cancer, smoking, and how to stop smoking, you can write to:

The American Cancer Society
4 West 35th Street
New York, NY 10001

For Further Reading

Books:

Friedberg, Errol C., editor. *Cancer Biology: Readings from Scientific American*. New York: W. H. Freeman, 1986.

Kupchella, Charles E. *Dimensions of Cancer*. Belmont, California: Wadsworth, 1987.

Special Issues of Periodicals:

"A Symposium—Cancer," in *Medical and Health Annual*, Encyclopædia Britannica, Chicago, 1981, including:

Shimkin, Michael B. "What Is Cancer?" pp. 76–89.

Wynder, Ernst. "Cancer Prevention," pp. 90–107.

Prout, Marianne N. and Swazey, Judith P. "The Impact of Cancer," pp. 108–119.

Canellos, George P. "Breast Cancer," pp. 120–133.

Moertel, Charles G. "Odyssey to the Unorthodox," pp. 134–147.

"Special Report: Cancer," in *Discover*, Volume 7, Number 3, March 1986, including:

Langone, John. "Cancer: Cautious Optimism," pp. 36–46.

Greenberg, Daniel S. "What Ever Happened to the War on Cancer?" pp. 47–64.

Thomas, Lewis. "Getting at the Roots of a Deep Puzzle," pp. 65–66.

Index

Page numbers in *italics* indicate illustrations.

About the Authors

Alvin and Virginia B. Silverstein have written over seventy books for young readers, mostly in the subject area of biological science. Their success is reflected in both reviews and awards—a number of their books, including the original edition of *Cancer*, have been cited as Outstanding Science Trade Books for Children by a joint committee from the National Science Teachers Association and the Children's Book Council.

Alvin Silverstein received his bachelor's degree from Brooklyn College, his master's degree from the University of Pennsylvania, and his doctorate from New York University. He is currently a professor of biology at the College of Staten Island of the City University of New York. Virginia B. Silverstein received her bachelor's degree from the University of Pennsylvania. She works as a translator of Russian scientific literature. They live in rural New Jersey.